Kissing Frogs

Enjoy and feel free to review on Amazon!

Rose Marie
Gloor

May 2019

TIPS AND TALES OF ONLINE DATING

ROSE MARIE GLOOR

RES PRESS • AUSTIN, TEXAS

Printed and bound by Bookmobile, Minneapolis

Copyright © 2016 by Rose Marie Gloor

Cover and book design by Emily Holke
Editing by Silvia de la Peña
www.KissingFrogsBook.com

Printed in the United States of America

For Greg – for planting the seed.
For Liz – for watering, fertilizing and manicuring.

The hardest thing I've ever done is keep believing
There's someone in this crazy world for me
The way that people come and go through temporary lives
My chance could come and I might never know

I used to say "No promises, let's keep it simple"
But freedom only helps you say goodbye
It took a while for me to learn that nothing comes for free
The price I paid is high enough for me

I know I need to be in love
I know I've wasted too much time
I know I ask perfection of a quite imperfect world
And fool enough to think that's what I'll find

So here I am with pockets full of good intentions
But none of them will comfort me tonight
I'm wide awake at four a.m.
Without a friend in sight
Hanging on to hope, but I'm alright

I know I need to be in love
I know I've wasted too much time
I know I ask perfection of a quite imperfect world
And fool enough to thing that's what I'll find

–The Carpenters, "I Need To Be In Love"

FOREWORD

How many Frogs does one girl have to kiss before she finds her Prince Charming? In my case, a whole stinking army of them! (You may not realize that an "army" of frogs is the actual term for a bunch of frogs. I may as well be accurate if I'm going to attempt to entertain you, right?) After finding myself on the unwanted receiving end of divorce papers right after turning 40, I decided to try online dating when I felt ready to consider finding a compatible mate. While not all of these Frogs were found hopping around online, the great majority of those I dated during a decade of being single throughout my 40s were met through one online dating service or another. I tried several different services, those that require payment to be a member and those that are free. It typically doesn't matter which one a person selects as most members are on multiple sites, I've found. I do personally believe that those who are on the sites that require payment may be more serious than others. Some people are lifetime members with no desire to end their membership ... ever. They go from girl to girl or guy to guy, year after year. There is nothing wrong with doing so, but one should just be upfront about it if they do intend to use a dating service in that manner. There are also those who are active online with the sole purpose of taking advantage of others. I will address that within these pages as well. The more informed a person can be, the better the overall online experience. That is the overall goal of this book – to share in the hopes that it will bring someone a better dating result than some of those I had.

So what makes me an expert on the subject of internet dating, you ask? Well, I'm not an expert actually. I don't believe anyone can be an expert in any type of dating as the game changes with each person, each email, each contact and every date. However, I've had enough personal experience to make me qualified to share a few of my own stories … the good, the bad and the downright ugly. I spent the better span of nine years exploring the available men online who caught my eye or considering those who were interested in me; what I have to share with you … well, you just can't make stuff like this up! The best stories always come from our own real life experiences.

Why do I think anyone would be interested in reading these stories? Oh, dear reader, let me count the ways. Within these pages that you hold in your hands, or are reading on your screen, are very intriguing and interesting characters right out of the story of my life. You will laugh, your mouth will drop open with shock and you may want to read parts of at least one of these chapters out loud to a friend. I will introduce you to liars, cheaters, brazen sex-crazed professionals and more. You will be introduced to a man who had issues with dog hair, another who stooped so low that he shouldn't be classified as a man, and I will invite you to join in the experience of a first kiss that will never leave your memory, and the crowning of Miss America. All these stories are compliments of my journey trying to find my Prince Charming online. Shall we continue?

Internet dating is an animal all its own complete with unknown, unwritten laws of the jungle; but really it's not completely unlike other forms of meeting people. It is simply another avenue to hopefully find that special someone, similar to attending a singles group at church, going to the dance club or walking through the frozen food aisle at the local grocery store. What? Oh, come on. Haven't you noticed all the men who hang out in the grocery store aisle where the air is the coldest? They push an almost empty cart, seem involved in finding something but are more interested in what is in your cart and checking out your ring hand. Take a look next time. They are there in hoards! I think it's actually some sort of secret club these particular men belong to ... but that's just me. Perhaps I'll ask next time I see one.

Nonetheless, back to the internet dating scene. It's a great way to meet someone you wouldn't have the opportunity to meet otherwise. It truly brings the radius of the larger dating world closer than it's ever been. There are roughly 40 million Americans participating in online dating services – that's roughly 40 percent of our U.S. single people population. What this could possibly mean for you or another interested party is an opportunity to meet someone with like-minded interests, goals, dreams and beliefs currently outside your own social circle and personal acquaintances. If you personally haven't tried online dating, you certainly must have an opinion about it. Someone in your group of friends or family has tried it either successfully or unsuccessfully. I truly know quite a few people who met their significant others online, including my sister who met her husband of 12 years on Match.com. Perhaps you are in a very happy relationship or have been married a very long time and just haven't decided if you want to keep your significant other yet. Either way, I hope you can enjoy these stories and be thankful they happened to me rather than to you.

I'd like to share with you readers some of the common sense type courtesies that I would enforce if I were the ultimate online dating site rule maker (as if there were such a thing). What many online daters don't realize is that these unwritten rules actually should be followed; unpublished dos and don'ts, along with certain common sense related courtesies of things that simply shouldn't be done or said. The issue is that there is no contract with rules to initial or an extensive legal document to sign when one joins a dating website. No one shares with you the rules of engagement. It is fair game and most of us, unfortunately, learn the hard way. I experienced many of the don'ts, but this eventually brought about the idea to share the results of my online encounters with you. Perhaps for laughs, or to have you shake your head and say to yourself, "Seriously?" Oh yes. If it's written in the pages of this book, it's a true story – it really, truly happened. Like I said, you can't make this kind of stuff up!

So, sit back, relax and let your mind wander. Share the fun, the laughs and, yes, the blatantly unbelievable through my personal experiences. Let me bring these guys to life on these pages, those who graced an hour, a day, or maybe longer in the book of my internet dating life. Pages behind me now, but time I won't ever get back. Time invested either foolishly, regretfully or happily. We will let these guys live forever in the print on these pages. Their names have been changed to prevent possible lawsuits for character defamation or hate mail coming my way (but perhaps just a letter here or there). Any genius who actively participated in part of this story of mine should be able to figure out if they made the book. At least there's that small token for all their efforts, right?

My hope is that when you are finished reading these pages, perhaps we will have shared a laugh, or you will have said the same four letter words I did, or maybe you will have come away with a different view of online dating. Perhaps of dating period. Because when it's all said and done, I truly believe there is someone out there for each of us. In fact, I'm a firm believer that there are several people out there for each of us. Some simply aren't put in our direct pathway in life. So, in order to change that, one must take a chance and do something different. The question, however, is whether we are willing to kiss enough Frogs to find that one Prince Charming who will brighten our world. Yes, I kissed a lot of Frogs during this time frame. Some good, some bad and some ugly. And, yes, in the end, I did find my Prince Charming – through a dating website.

ACKNOWLEDGMENTS

I absolutely loved writing this book and enjoyed the creative process immensely. The hours flew by when I was lost in my world of creating this for my enjoyment and those of future readers. While I kept this project secret from my friends and family during the year and a half it took me to complete, there were a few special people who participated in one way or another who I would like to sincerely thank:

My sister Liz Asay in Montana. You were there with me from the beginning when the seed was planted. Asking questions, encouraging every step, laughing with me and prodding my progress. You were my first reader, my first editor and my first fan. Thank you for being there during the many months it took for me to complete! You made a difference and I love you for being there every chapter.

My former co-workers and girlfriends, Emily Holke and Silvia de la Peña. You two are the most talented marketing team that I am blessed to know. When I asked Emily if she would design my book cover, she gladly agreed and then volunteered Silvia to help with editing and providing input for creativity and publishing. Little did I know that they both had awesome talents and experience that made this project so much easier than it would have been without them! We three became lunch buddies and had a grand time laughing about the online experiences they both have had and comparing them to mine in this book. I valued their input, expertise, and help with editing, formatting and marketing. Without these two ladies to help with this project, it may not have ever gone to print. I owe them a debt I can never repay. They are very special to me and I adore them! Thank you both so much.

Although I've never met her, my sincere thanks to Emily's Aunt Cheryl who read my first manuscript while they were on vacation together. Cheryl read the book in one day on the beach and laughed out loud while she enjoyed the stories and read excerpts to her friend. While never a member of online dating (she's been married for many, many years), she enjoyed the book very much, which warmed my heart and confirmed that the audience for these stories goes beyond online daters.

Finally, my Prince Charming and supportive husband, Robert. When I shared with you that I was going to write a book, you encouraged me. You let me pack my computer on every trip, invest hours every holiday and spend weekends devoting time to my project. Not once did you mutter the words, "Are you working on that thing again?!" You even put up with my sudden outbursts of laughter when I wrote something that tickled my fancy. I love you for supporting my passion to put these stories in print and I admire your willpower to wait until the book was in print before reading them. You are Mr. Unbelievable and I am blessed to share this life with you. (Although you did say it gave you some concern that I dated enough men to fill up an entire book!)

Last but not least – thank you to those readers who are currently holding these pages, those who took a chance on reading my book. I hope you enjoyed the journey and came away smiling. If I succeeded in that small task, it was all worth it. Every date. Every Frog. Every kiss.

CONTENTS

DO NOT LIE, PERIOD

When a person decides to join an internet dating website, they have to make a personal choice if they intend to be open and honest in who they truly are and who they will present to those who may possibly be interested. That means if they are of a certain age, height, weight, marital status or financial situation ... do they choose to list reality, or is this a time for fantasy, games and make believe? As these areas are the most common that dating hopefuls tend to exaggerate or flat out lie about when participating in online dating, a conscious decision takes place to be upfront or stretch the truth. For example, he may be 5′9″ but, oh gosh, doesn't 5′11″ or 6′ sound so much more desirable to a potential mate? Because she would have to be an idiot to notice he isn't actually that height in real life if they meet in person, right? Ummm, right. But I'm getting ahead of myself. That story is still to come.

On some of the more popular dating websites, each person fills out a personal profile consisting of categories including age, occupation, marital status, number of children, and details about personal appearance. Besides listing height, they are usually required to select a body style or shape. It gives the person previewing the profile an opportunity to choose those attributes that appeal to them the most. It's kind of like car shopping when one looks for a prospective date online; he or she selects a sleek, smooth, long frame with the curves in all the right places, like a Jaguar XK or a Porsche. But imagine if on the big day of delivery, up drives a chubby little VW Bug. Wait! How does that happen, anyway? Well, because the person filling out the online dating profile doesn't tell the truth, you see. If you decide to participate in online dating and the choices are Thin, Average, Athletic, Curvy, or A Few Extra Pounds in relation to body type, be extremely accurate in the description of yourself. Unless you have no plans to meet the person you are communicating with, they will find out soon enough. So, be honest with yourself and with the person who may be interested in you. Don't answer the questions based on who you want to be. This should always be about who you actually are at that very moment in time. After all, this is real life dating, not fantasy.

People may stretch the truth about many aspects of who they are. Yes, there are even married men and women posing as available suitors online. If their marital status says "Separated," I recommend avoiding them until that status changes. The separation is usually more within their mind and heart, not in reality. A sure fire test of whether or not someone is 100 percent available is if they can't be reached by phone or text in the evenings and weekends, or if they use the excuse, "I live with roommates" when you want to see their place. Real roommates don't mind visitors, but spouses have a whole different opinion about that sort of thing. If you are still in a relationship – regardless of how committed either of you are to each other or how close to ending it is – you shouldn't be active on a dating website. It's not fair to those who are truly available. Get finished with your business before inviting others into a possible mess. Nobody wants an angry spouse texting back with, "Who the hell is this and can you tell me exactly why you are texting my husband!?"

Don't get me started on the posting of accurate or rather inaccurate photos. Let me ask this – do we women walk around every day looking like we stepped out of a glamour shot portrait? No, we don't! So why would someone use that type of photo as their only profile picture? Unless she plans to stop by to have someone do her makeup and hair right before the first date, it might be a wise idea to post realistic, untouched, natural photos of who she really is. Otherwise, isn't it a form of lying? Likewise, if you are a guy, post some close up photos that truly show you up close. And get rid of the hat and sunglasses, buster. Let's be fair, shall we? One other bit of advice – don't post photos of your friends or family unless you have their permission to do so. Common courtesy.

In the big wide world of internet dating, we can each be whoever we want to be behind the safety of our computer monitors. If that means stretching the truth or lying or being unfaithful, well, that's fine. Not really, but each person makes that decision for themselves. At some point, however, we each will take a chance and get out from behind the safety of that computer screen and meet a few people face to face. My hope for you is that you won't have to do some explaining or justifying or clarifying when that time comes. Consider being you. Don't stretch the truth and don't lie. It never ends well.

One of the worst experiences I was told involving blatant lying was shared with me by a guy I met as we exchanged horror stories of online dating during dinner. That's what we online daters like to do on dates with other online daters. Tell horror stories about other dates we've had. This guy told me how a woman he was very interested in posted a photo of her younger sister on her dating profile instead of using a photo of herself. He was very interested in this woman, or actually with the woman he thought he was writing to and investing his time communicating with. When he showed up for that first dinner date, imagine his surprise when he didn't see the beautiful woman from the photo waiting for him. Instead, he was greeted by someone older, heavier and less attractive. He felt betrayed when this woman admitted the photo she used was of her sister, and rightfully so. Would you believe she then asked him to stay and have dinner with her since they were both there anyway? Of course, he didn't stay. Additionally, he told this woman she needed to be herself and stop using her sister's photo on her online profile as it was extremely deceitful, to say the least. Needless to say, this experience gave this particular guy a very bad impression about women being honest online. He was quite pleased that my photos looked exactly like I did in real life. I restored his faith somewhat in women online. Please. Always use your own photo.

Another story I was told recently of a woman's worst internet date ever was a guy who she was very interested in, who lied on his dating profile and, ultimately, to her. It seems that after several dates and time spent together, he finally decided it was a good opportunity to clear the air and share. This man stated on his dating profile that he had no children. One night at dinner over candlelight and wine, he admitted that he had four children. With four different women. How in God's name did this man ever think that this would turn out well for him? Was he completely brain dead? He had four children! Count them. One, two, three and four. Maybe none of them lived with him, but the fact remained that he had four children. This woman shared with me that she got up from the table and walked out. She left him during dinner and never spoke to him again. Lying is lying is lying. Simple as that.

My own personal favorite story involving all sorts of deceit and lying was one of my very first online dates. It was very early in my online dating experience and I had just one single encounter with this person (sometimes one can be enough). I can't even remember his real name. But I do remember what he told me – what I thought was the truth and what were actually his lies. The experience made quite an impression on me early and in some ways helped me to distinguish between what was likely true and not so true with future potential dates. I at least knew what to watch out for and which questions to ask up front. So, my first experience with lies and the confessing of those lies went something like this.

Let's call him 007, which will make sense shortly. Actually, let's call him James. James "Not So" Bond (cue the spy movie music). James and I hit it off very quickly online. He was friendly and playful in his approach and I found him to be intriguing. He only posted one photo on his profile but it was a close up of his face (however, he was also wearing aviator sunglasses) and he was wearing a black T-shirt. I admit I thought it extremely odd that he didn't show his eyes, but he had a nice smile and I decided I wanted to meet him. Per his online dating profile, James was 47 years old, divorced, had no children that he spoke of and was recently retired from the government. Military, maybe? At that time, I was 42, retired military, lived in his general proximity and was recently divorced as well. We seemed to be compatible in several ways. I was very excited to meet him! The date couldn't come quick enough.

We planned to meet at 7:30 on a Friday night at a local Mexican restaurant, and I was quite nervous when I pulled into the parking lot. I got there way too early but sat in my car trying to calm my nerves and continuously checked my lipstick (as if it would change from minute to minute). Right at 7:29, I got out of my car and strolled across the parking lot. Walking towards the entrance door, I saw James standing there looking exactly as I remembered him from his photo. How clever was that, I thought? How could I not recognize him? Black T-shirt, aviator sunglasses and a big smile. I walked towards him with butterflies in my stomach. It's natural to have butterflies when you're meeting someone you've been communicating with, are excited to finally meet and seem to share some interests with. Who knows, he could be The One, right? This Frog might actually be your very own Prince Charming! Will he be what you expected? More importantly, will you be what he expected? Hence the butterflies.

"Rose?" he said as he extended his hand towards me.

"James?" I returned as I clasped his hand and looked at my reflection in those shiny, mirror-like sunglasses. Ahhh, my lipstick still looked fabulous. Wait! Why was he wearing sunglasses when the sun had almost set and he was standing in the shade by the restaurant? It was almost dark out there. 'Oh, shut up,' I told myself. 'Who really cares? I'm here. He's here. Let's get this party started!'

"Shall we?" James said as he opened the door to the restaurant and finally removed his sunglasses.

I sneaked a look his way to get a quick glance at this mystery man's full face. As I entered the restaurant, I thought to myself, 'How old did he say he was?'

As we were led to our table by the waitress, my mind tried to grasp the age of the face I saw briefly as we entered. He did not look quite as young as I thought he should. Something was just not right.

Sitting down across from James in the booth, I finally got a really good look at him. He was an attractive man but he sure looked older than I expected him to, which was evident in the lines and wrinkles around his eyes. In fact, he looked quite weathered. Was that why he wore the sunglasses in his photo and again when he showed up that night? Why did he want to hide that? 'Is he embarrassed about his looks?' I wondered. He may have looked older than I thought he would, but he was still very attractive.

The waiter came by and took our order for drinks – margaritas for us both, and we finally began our first date. We made small talk about the restaurant, he complimented me on how closely I resembled my profile photos and the waitress delivered our drinks.

"Cheers," we said as we clinked our frosty glasses. The next words from James were unexpected and certainly got my attention.

"I need to confess that a few things weren't quite accurate on my profile, before we go any further," he said.

Wait, what? This didn't sound good.

"Oh? Just how far from the truth was your profile information, James?" I replied as I pushed myself back from the table and gave him my best "this better be good, mister" look. I really don't like to be deceived. 'Married, maybe? He better not be,' I thought. 'I may be tempted to make a scene.'

"Well, I am not just retired from the government, and unlike you, it wasn't from the military. I actually retired from the CIA," he said.

Well, that wasn't so bad, was it? A CIA agent! My own secret agent right there in the flesh! That was kind of exciting. That would've made me one of those Bond girls in the 007 movies with the sexy untamed hair, skin-tight dress, pouty lips and gun tucked up somewhere private. (No pun intended.) But, oh, it appeared he wasn't done confessing. I focused back on James.

"I'm also not 47 years old," he continued.

Really? Now I knew why he didn't want to use a photo taken without those shiny aviator sunglasses. His face certainly did show his age, especially around the eyes.

"Okay, James, I'll bite," I said. "Again, how far from the truth did you happen to get?"

He looked at me across the table, took a deep breath and said, "I'm 52."

Ummm, let's see. Basic math skills at work here. He was really 52 years old, not 47 like I believed him to be – because he had put 47 on his profile and why would I think he would lie? I was 42 years old, which I didn't lie about.

That made him 10 years older than me, which wasn't a deal breaker, but what was a potential problem was that he had lied. I don't like being lied to. But wait, he still wasn't done? One moment, please ... I needed to take a big drink of my margarita!

James looked across the table at me and said, "And I have a two-year-old son that I share custody of with my ex-wife. But that's it. Everything else was true, I promise. So, here I am and the night is young. Right, Rose? There. I feel so much better now that you know the truth. So, what do you think?" he smiled.

Lovely. What did I think? Well, I truly do try my best to avoid using profane language in public places, around children or at least until after the third drink – except inside my own head with me, myself and I. 'I better think about this and possibly filter the message before I speak,' I thought. He wasn't 47 years old, he wasn't retired military (which didn't matter) but to add insult to injury, he also had a very small child. My situation was this: I had a teenage son getting ready to graduate from high school in a few years, and this man was just beginning to raise a family with an ex-wife who probably loathed him and wanted to make his life a living hell. Why? Because the man was clearly deceptive! He was a liar! Just perfect. Simply. Perfect.

Oh, was it my turn to speak now? James stared at me expecting a response. 'Be nice,' I tell myself, 'because he's going to pay for your dinner and drinks – and right now I need another one.'

"Well, first let me ask you a question," I said very amicably. "Why on earth would you lie about your age, James?"

He shrugged and replied, "Because all the women I'm interested in online are looking for a man between the ages of 38 and 49 years old. If I put my real age on my profile, it would remove me from their search results."

Oh, right. So why not lie about your age so you can meet women who still want suitors under the age of 49 – and news flash, you aren't! But, naturally, you would still be a liar. It doesn't take a rocket scientist to realize that this plan isn't going to work. If you are 52 years old, face it. You. Are. 52. Years. Old!

"Oh? Really?" I said just a tiny bit sarcastically. "What did my profile say? What age group of men am I interested in on my profile, James?"

He shook his head and admitted he didn't know.

I informed him that my profile, if he wanted to go back and take a closer look, listed the age range of 38-60 years old. Therefore, he would have fit within my preferences perfectly without lying at all. I followed this up with, "And as I look across the table at this moment listening to you, I will now question every single word you say to me. I will be asking myself, 'Is he telling me the truth?' I will wonder if this certain part or that part is a lie. I'll think, 'Did you really do that?' I won't be able to trust or believe anything you say from this moment forward." I took a long, satisfying drink of my margarita and smiled.

James didn't return the smile.

Needless to say, he was very quiet during the rest of dinner, which didn't last very long after that point. We ordered food, we ate, finished our drinks and made friendly conversation. We said our goodbyes in the parking lot and very shortly after returning home, I received an email from James that said thanks for meeting him but he didn't think we needed to continue our communication as there was no spark between us. Yes, I agreed. It's a funny thing how being called a liar in a subtle way or someone telling you lies can take the spark right out of any potential relationship. I didn't reply.

Another first date experience with an over exaggerated sense of reality (come on, let's call it what it is – a bold faced lie) on a guy's profile that was also very disappointing to me was with meeting Bryan. I typically didn't seriously consider or show any interest in anyone shorter than I am. It's not that I'm opposed to dating guys my height, but it's because I like wearing three to five inch heels. Given that I'm 5'7", once you slap a nice, sexy pair of four-inch hooker heels on my feet, I'm now 5'11". It takes a very confident man to stand next to a woman in heels towering over him. More men are opposed to this height difference than are actually in favor of it. They lack a certain machismo, apparently. So when I started getting fun emails from Bryan, I hesitated a little bit. His profile showed that he was 5'7", so we were the same height if I wore flat shoes. Flat shoes! You may as well beat me to a bloody pulp and hang me out to bleed to death on a clothesline. It would be torture to wear flat shoes to a first date! But Bryan was a cutie pie and I hadn't had many dates as of yet, so I figured I might as well meet him. I mean, who knew? Maybe he was The One. And surely he realized we were the same height, so he wouldn't lie about something like that, right? Sigh. Read on.

Bryan and I met Saturday afternoon for a late lunch

date at a location between our respective neighborhoods. I thought I had gotten there early, but he beat me to the restaurant and was already waiting at the table when I walked in.

The waitress showed me to Bryan's table, which was raised up on a platform about a foot. I'm sure you know the type I am describing. Booths that are cozy but require you to step up to get into the seating area. So when he stood up to greet me, I thought, 'I so could have worn something other than these ugly flats!'

Until, that is, Bryan stepped off the upraised portion of our booth's seating area to greet me. And there I was … looking directly at the top of his forehead – at his hairline, to be exact. We didn't even look eye to eye! Do you know how much shorter than you someone has to be in order to look at their hairline? Oh my good God. I doubt that he was even 5'4". Why!? How did he think this was possible? If I am not lying about my height (and why would I?), but he starts off with a lie, wouldn't this man have foreseen an issue when we actually met? Yes, he was nice looking and, yes, he was interesting. But, no, he was not even close to being 5'7" and, therefore, he lied. We finished our lunch and that was that. I resisted the urge to sing, "Liar, liar, pants on fire" when we said goodbye. Sigh.

Don't get me wrong. Women lie and stretch the truth as well about many things. But it never turns out well in the end. There will always be that moment when the confession or realization takes place that honesty was not part of that person's core value system. I laughingly told my girlfriends that men always seem to add inches. They can't help it.

They just do. They add inches to the fish they catch. To their height, apparently. And as we know, other places. I'm sorry. I'm just writing what you were already thinking. And you guessed correctly if you wondered if Bryan and I only had that one date. Had I known he was that much shorter than I was, we never would have had the first one. Had he been honest about his profile, yes, if only – but too often, profiles contain only parts of the truth. Not who we are in reality but who we want to be. This is lying and, again, I stress, it never turns out well.

This brings me to my very first online date. While he didn't lie about anything, it was interesting how he afforded me the opportunity to bow out gracefully without lying. We met at a Dairy Queen near our homes and after spending time together, he asked me a very direct question.

"You have been divorced for only a year, Rose, and you just started dating. I've been single for several years and I'm ready to find my life partner and settle down. Are you?"

This man was attractive, successful and interesting. I could have easily lied and said yes and continued to see him for many months. However, the truth was simply this – I was a victim of a recent hurtful divorce that I didn't want. I was not ready to settle down regardless of how wonderful this man was. The right thing to do right then was to say exactly that, which is what I did. I told the truth. We went our own ways and I experienced many other dates – some good and some bad. Hopefully, he found who he was looking for and lived happily ever after. We were both honest with each other from the beginning and that is exactly how it should always be.

My final thought before moving on to more online dating stories is to encourage all members of dating websites to not use these forums for entertainment purposes only. I'm not proud to admit that I did that off and on for quite some time during the first few years. As I don't watch television, I would spend my evenings communicating with several guys who were looking for their potential mate. I had no intention of meeting any of them at that point in time. I just wanted to fill a void in my life and truly avoided having a real date at all costs. If they forced the issue, I simply stopped emailing or talking to them. This wasn't fair to any of these gentleman who were interested in me. I remember laughingly telling my mom when I would visit her that I needed to answer my "fan mail" each evening – in other words, my email correspondence on the dating websites that I was a member of. It wasn't until one of these guys I was writing to during that particular timeframe asked me point blank if I had any intention of ever meeting him, or was I using online dating for "entertainment purposes" only? It was then that I realized how wrong I was, because while my profile stated I was interested in meeting my Prince Charming, my actions were not sincere and told a very different story. In essence, I was lying. I share the outcome of that realization later in this book.

Simply put, don't lie about who you are when you fill out your online dating profile. Additionally, be completely honest about why you are participating in online dating. We are who we are, as I said earlier. The good, the bad and sometimes maybe even the ugly. But isn't it better to be honest and have that potential Prince Charming be very happy that the person they are interested in truly is who their profile said they were? If you start out with lies, sooner or later you'll have to confess. That never turns out well for either party. It says so much about who we each are in other areas of our life than stretching the truth is truly worth. You will always, and I mean always, be faced with telling the truth eventually. Trust me. 🐾

BE INTERESTED –
NOT JUST INTERESTING

When you meet someone and are truly interested in them, it's important that they are also truly interested in you. Conversation between two people who meet should be a back and forth proposition. If one person is doing all the sharing while the other person sits there smiling and nodding, something is wrong.

I like to think of communication between two people not unlike giving and receiving gifts. I pass the gift to someone, they hold it for a little while and share themselves with me, and then they gladly pass it back to me so that I can also share. I tell of my upbringing for a minute or two. He either asks questions, to which I respond and continue talking, or I stop after a little while and ask him a question. It's at that point I'm passing the gift back to him. If he is truly interested in learning about me, he will answer my question and share a bit more before he passes that gift right back to me by asking another question. If he holds the gift, talks only of himself and asks no questions about me, he isn't interested in me. He's interested in himself and wants me to be interested in him also. Some people are looking for a fan club rather than a possible mate, and they don't like sharing in a two-way exchange of communication. It's also important that the conversation be appropriate for the moment and comfortable for both parties.

I once met a Frog online who I was much more interested in and initially impressed with than he was with me. This particular Frog happened to be an attorney, a corporate attorney, and he was very smooth and polished. I have to admit that the thought of dating an attorney had some appeal, yes. An educated and professional man – that held my interest, for a minute.

His name was Sam and he couldn't have lived further away from me and still have been in the same city. Because of the difference between our homes, we agreed to meet on a weeknight after work. We met for dinner halfway between our respective homes after chatting online for only a few days. Sam invited me to join him at a very nice, upscale restaurant in town one evening and I was extremely excited to meet him. I liked how he looked in his business suit the first time we met and he had a very suave demeanor. He was waiting at the entrance to the restaurant when I arrived and, after making introductions, we went inside and were shown to our table complete with candlelight and an aura of romance. I was impressed!

This guy was the essence of a corporate attorney. Nice suit, great tie, fabulous hair and an engaging smile. Sam ordered wine and appetizers for both of us. He seemed extremely at ease and I enjoyed being part of the moment. Until, that is, the dinner conversation began after toasting to good health with our wine glasses. Sam was a great communicator; however, he only wanted to discuss two things: Sam and sex, and not necessarily in that order. Well, sometimes the subject was just about Sam, and then it would transfer to being only about sex, and a few times it was about both Sam and sex.

What an odd conversation this turned out to be for a

first dinner date. Sam wasn't interested in who I was. No questions about my job or my family or upbringing. The whole conversation was centered on how wonderful Sam was (in and out of bed) and how tough his job as a corporate attorney could be. The late nights he worked, his recent divorce and how those hours played into that happening. And then it would switch to how he was looking for someone who would be experimental and adventurous during sex. Wait! I wasn't even sure I wanted to see this guy again, and he was already asking me if I was adventurous. I was appalled!

Then the unreal became nightmarish. Sam looked at me over his wine glass with a smoldering gaze. "Would you consider having sex with me on a huge beach ball?" he asked.

I almost choked on a piece of my steak tartar. Really? Was this actually happening? Sam was waiting for an answer regarding the beach ball question while I wondered if I had stepped into the Twilight Zone. How awkward was this moment? I glanced to the left to see if the people at the table closest to us were listening to our conversation. They didn't appear to be, but it didn't make it any less uncomfortable. Sex on a beach ball? Where had this come from and why was I even thinking about it?

I'm not even sure what I said, but somehow I avoided the question about the beach ball sex act and the dinner continued. Sam also continued to brag about his career, his house, his interest in strange sexual activities.

As dinner continued, I couldn't get the thought of the huge beach ball out of my mind. How embarrassing would that be to get bucked off and thrown to the ground during the heat of the moment? I could dislocate a shoulder, or a pelvic bone for that matter. I just wasn't sure I was athletic enough to look sexy, act sexy, sound sexy and try to stay on a beach ball all at the same time. Not to mention that I was certain Sam intended to be offering some sort of force or friction against me and the beach ball, which would have made balance even all the more difficult! Why was I even having these thoughts? I should have been concentrating on Sam, who was certainly sharing how wonderful he was with yours truly.

It occurred to me that we hadn't talked about Rose once during this dinner. Not once. Well, except to ask if I had any interest in having sex on a big, oversized beach ball, that is. This simply wasn't cool. How could I get out of this situation and stop thinking about the beach ball? I came back to the present moment to hear Sam sharing about his ex-wife.

"She just wasn't experimental enough," he said. "She wouldn't consider having sex on the balcony of our hotel on our last vacation together. Okay, so it was daytime and other people were out on their balconies as well. But where was her sense of fun and adventure?"

Oh dear God, this guy wasn't who I thought he was. I somehow thought that an attorney might have been a little more professional on the first date, and might in some way have been interested in me. But no, he was not interested in me at all. Sam was interested in Sam and wanted me to be as well. The thought occurred to me that if he was having this conversation with me on our first date, he was having it with other women on their first dates with him also. While those other women may have been impressed with Sam, the corporate attorney with his nice house south of town, this girl wasn't interested. I couldn't wait for the evening to end so I could put Sam in the loser bucket and move on to someone who was actually interested in me and asked questions specifically about me. Someone who wanted to share information about himself, but could hold an appropriate dinner conversation that didn't include sex on oversized beach balls.

The dinner ended, we walked outside to the street, Sam promised to call and I thanked him for an interesting evening. He kissed my cheek and hugged me close.

"Think about that beach ball, Rose," he whispered warmly in my ear. "It will change your life."

I bit my tongue and thanked him for dinner. As I drove home, I couldn't get the conversation out of my mind, and how very inappropriate it was. No interest in me unless I was willing to try out my athletic prowess on the big beach ball. And I guessed eight seconds wasn't what Sam had in mind! I had hoped I could meet someone who would be interested in me, not just in sharing who they were. Unfortunately, this was not to be my only experience with a Frog who was more interested in himself than they were with me. At least the next one didn't ask me about having sex on an oversized beach ball.

Terry lived in an upscale golfing community in the same town I lived in. We wrote to each other for a few weeks and he wanted to meet. Terry was a detective on the local police force and was very attractive. I agreed to come over to his house one Friday night so that we could go out to dinner together. I admit that his house was impressive from the outside although I didn't go inside after I arrived. Terry met me at the door, we got into his Cadillac and drove to dinner downtown. He was very interested in sharing with me during the trip to the restaurant how much money he made, how important he was in the community and brag about how many women he had dated.

As we approached the restaurant, Terry asked, "Have you ever been to the VIP room at the Gold Club?" I told him that I had not and he explained how difficult it was to get in.

He was truly out to impress me as after a very expensive dinner, we ended up in that VIP room at the Gold Club. He seemed to know everyone, especially all the ladies. We got the royal treatment with champagne and a private seating area that overlooked the dance floor. He seemed very proud to have shared the moment with me.

I wasn't impressed. Terry told me so many things about himself and his wonderful life but he wasn't interested enough to ask one question about me. Not one question. I felt completely out of place in his world, alone on that first date and knew that it would be the last.

When we returned to his house, Terry took me into his arms on the driveway and whispered, "Would you like to come inside to see my house and enjoy a nightcap?"

I refused. Somehow I believed that there may have been an expectation of repayment for that date. I had no intention to spend one more moment with a Frog who was more interested in himself than in getting to know me. Unfortunately, Terry wasn't the only Frog in this category or my future.

Take Erick, for example. He was so excited to meet me after we spoke on the phone that I caved in and decided to go out on a "school night" (that's what I say when I have to work the next day). I agreed to meet him for a pre-determined, limited amount of time at a combination upscale restaurant and dance club, although we never ate or danced after I arrived. In fact, we never got past the lobby. We did drink a beer in a little reception area where there was an overstuffed sofa. We sat for about an hour and a half – Erick talking and me listening. Oh, he was entertaining and he had stories. I listened for the allotted 90 minutes I had agreed to spend with him and then I went home. He didn't want me to leave, begged me to stay all the way out to my car and finally said goodbye with a promise to call me to arrange for another date. While driving home, I wondered if Erick truly was as shallow as he first appeared, realizing he knew nothing about me (except what I posted on my online profile), and he hadn't seemed like he wanted to find out. This left me feeling unsatisfied and empty. He did make me laugh, though, so I decided I would give him another chance if he asked me out again. He was, after all, nice looking and very funny. I tend to have a warped sense of humor, so anyone who makes me laugh is worth a second try.

One thing that people who are only interested in themselves tend to do is seek out others who will listen intently as they share how wonderful they are, how they grew up and every other detail they care to share. So it shouldn't have been a surprise that Erick called me in a few short days and wanted to go to dinner the following weekend. I decided it couldn't hurt to try again. Maybe I had been too hard on him and he would be more attentive this time.

We met close to my neighborhood and he was so happy to see me. As you might already expect, I learned so much more about Erick on that date. How he had a serious surgery a few years ago, the fact that he grew up in San Antonio with 10 siblings and that he was very close to his mother. He was nice to look at, but I became very bored. My mind wandered and I lost interest. It wasn't difficult to make the decision that I didn't want to see him again. The date ended, he exclaimed what a great time he had and said he hoped we could do it again very soon. Sure, right. Yawn.

'I'll need to wash my hair that night,' I thought. Or perhaps my sister would need my help cleaning out her cat's litter box. I've always been good at digging those clumps of kitty poop out of the litter without spilling it everywhere. It sure beat listening to another chapter in the book of Erick.

It wasn't but a few days later that Erick called me at work to see if I would be interested in going out with him the following Friday night. It wasn't a school night and I had no plans, so I was certainly available but completely uninterested. I can still remember that call, where I was standing in my office, the scenery I was looking at out the office window as I listened to him, and every word I said in return. Memories where we take a stand for the principles we believe in are like that. The ones that mean something to us personally are forever engrained in our minds. This conversation meant something to me, as it was probably one of the easiest ones I've had while communicating a very difficult message. I felt very strongly that I was worth waiting for someone who was interested in me. I just wasn't willing to invest any more of my life on someone who wasn't interested in getting to know me.

When Erick asked if I'd be available to go out that Friday evening, I replied with conviction that I was not interested. He was stunned.

"What?! Why not? We had such a wonderful time together and enjoyed each other's company so much!" he said. "Why in the world would you not be interested?"

"Because, Erick, I know everything about you," I said. "However, you know absolutely nothing about me after many phone conversations and two dates."

Did he truly not realize exactly how shallow and selfish he was?

"What? I know about you! What do you mean I know nothing about you?" he stammered.

Oh, this was going to be entertaining. 'I'll play your silly game, Erick,' I thought. 'May I have the category Clueless for $100, please? Well, yes you may, Rose.'

"Okay, Erick. I know where you work, I know where you grew up, I know that you have ten siblings and you are the youngest child. I also know about your surgery. Do tell. What do you truly know about me?" I said, and then I waited. Knowing.

"I know where you work and I know about your kids," said the clueless, soon-to-be former, potential person of interest.

Wow. He knew where I worked. But did he say kids?

As in more than one? Like two kids or more? Plural? I was extremely curious.

"Really, Erick? You know how many kids I have? Tell me then. How many kids do I have? What are their names? How old are they? I want to hear this," I replied with no hope of receiving the right answer, if any answer at all. Erick had just stepped into a big trap and the sharp lid had snapped shut.

There was nothing but silence on the other end of the line. Maybe he needed some encouragement to actually admit he was clueless.

"Well, Erick? Do tell, really. How many kids do I have?"

You might think that Erick actually knew, or that he guessed and threw out a number. Maybe he would even get it right, but he was a little smarter than that. No guess is better than the wrong guess. He admitted that he had no idea. However, he pleaded with me to give him another chance, go out on another date, let him learn about me and tell him how many kids I have. He wanted to know everything about me now. But now was simply too late.

Instead, I told Erick that I needed to let him go. I was releasing him back into the dating stream for someone else to consider. This was a catch and release experience. He simply was not a keeper. I then told Erick something I will always remember, and I'm certain he will as well. If more women would treat themselves with the respect they deserve and hold their heads high while refusing to settle for someone not interested in them, there would be many more women repeating these words that I shared with Erick before I said goodbye and hung up on him. Never were words truer and more deeply deserved.

"Erick, you just aren't good enough for me. I deserve so much more than you will ever be. Goodbye." Click. Then I smiled knowing I was absolutely right in doing so.

When I've shared this story with friends, they are shocked and can't believe I'd tell a guy that. Why not? It was true. I was not willing to settle. We each only get 24 single hours in a day, no more, no less. If I spend an hour with someone who isn't interested in me, I can't get that time back. Look at that time spent with someone else as an investment. Don't waste it if there is no possibility of receiving dividends. I'm not referring to monetary rewards. Invest in people who are interested in you, spend your time with those willing to share themselves and truly want you to do the same. Share your minutes, your hours and your days with someone who really wants to know you and sincerely cares about who you are. Anyone can make himself or herself interesting, but can they also be interested in you at the same time? Choose to invest your moments with someone who is interested. This is true in all aspects of your life. You are so very worth it. 🐾

MORE THAN A GREAT PRE-PACKAGED DEAL

There are those online who are looking for a certain type of mate that might not necessarily align with your idea of true love and romance. We all want to find that one person who lights up our eyes when they enter the room, who takes our breath away and makes our heart beat a little bit faster, don't we? Is that realistic or just a fairy tale? I believe these life partners actually do exist, and good for you if you were lucky enough to find that person in your life. What I found with online dating is that there are several categories of interest. Some people are interested in the fairy tale, others are interested in some sort of companionship, and perhaps others are interested in making their lives easier financially, or otherwise more comfortable, through what the other person has to offer. I'm referring to both men and women in this category.

I once met a guy who was interested in me, but with a definite agenda of his own. Unfortunately, his agenda didn't mesh well with mine in the long run.

George was a handsome guy who was sweet and charming when he wanted to be. We had fun together on our first few dates and I noticed that he was a perfectionist, similar to myself. We were quite compatible until I met his kids. Remember, it's a package deal, and if someone has kids, they are clearly part of the overall package. If you have kids, keep in mind that someone else will have to consider whether or not your total package gels with their wants and wishes as well. Not only are your kids part of the package, but your ex-spouse and the relationship you share with them are also. Yes, it can be messy, but it doesn't stop us from wanting to find that special person, does it? We just have to be sure we are getting what we are truly looking for.

The first time I met George's kids, they joined us for a late fall day trip out to the lake to spend an afternoon on his boat. Two pre-teens, one girl and one boy, sitting in the backseat of the truck staring at me like I was some kind of bug splattered on the windshield. Non-responsive, unfriendly and uninterested in anything I had to offer. In that aspect, meeting someone with little kids might have been easier. But I was not interested in raising anyone else's children as my son, a senior in high school, was almost out of the house. However, I got to see the interaction between a father and his kids as I shared that day with all of them. That alone can be a great indicator of the dynamics in the relationship your potential future mate shares with his own children. It speaks volumes about the harmony or disharmony you will be entering as a potential life participant.

In this particular case, George fussed at his kids when they put their feet up on his seats, yelled at them during our boat ride and complained about how expensive their meals were when we stopped to eat. Clearly the weekends with his kids were not chock full of bonding and good times. I was never so glad to return to my quiet, empty house that evening, greeted only by my dog. A place where I didn't have to experience the stress of trying to fit into an already tense situation between a part-time father and his kids. Oh, but that's not where this story ends.

A classic indication that George was more interested in what I had to offer rather than truly wanting to be with me came the first time I invited him over to my house. I was very proud of the home I bought, lived in with my teenage son and took great care of. I spent hours in my yard landscaping, had invested in upgrading the interior and, while modest, it was a very nice two-story home. There were four bedrooms, two and a half baths and a nice deck in the back. I'm sure it was quite a change from George's very small, two-bedroom, and one bath apartment that he disliked, compliments of a nasty divorce and meager financial means due to his monthly child support responsibilities.

The afternoon George walked into my house for the first time will dwell in my mind as a classic memory. I saw him arrive as I stood in the kitchen gazing out the bay windows; he couldn't see me due to the solar screens. He walked up my driveway, gazing up into the large trees in the front yard, admiring the flowers in the beds along the sidewalk and smiling as he approached the front door. The doorbell rang, I opened the front door and invited him inside.

After giving me a hug, George stepped further into the room and began to take it all in.

"Would you like a tour of the house?" I asked.

He was most eager and interested. After showing George the upstairs, downstairs and yard, we returned to the main part of the house. Looking around the living room, walking into the kitchen with its large bay windows that looked out onto the beautifully landscaped front yard, he began to nod his head.

I began to smile, feeling quite pleased that he found my house so impressive. Oh yes, I was patting myself on this "I-N-D-E-P-E-N-D-E-N-T, do you know what I mean" single woman's back. I had confirmation that I had indeed done a great job with my home improvement projects. I was feeling proud, you can understand. I loved my house and it appeared that George did, too. Little did I know what that smile was truly all about and why those little wheels inside his head were turning so feverishly! He enlightened me. Oh yes, he did. And here is how he did just that.

"This is really nice, Rose," George said as he continued to look around the living room, nodding. "Very nice. Actually, this will work out just fine for me."

Uh oh. Something about the way he made the words "just" and "fine" drag on in a sing song-y fashion made the hair on the back of my neck stand up. Come again?

"Yes, this will work out juuuusst fiiine for me," he repeated.

I knew I would regret asking this, but how could I leave such a statement hanging out there in the air like that? Now the hair on my arms was also standing at attention. "Oh? How so?" I asked, feeling a little confused.

Here it came. "Well, my apartment lease ends in a few months. I can just move right in here with you – there's plenty of room. I'll pay you about $500 a month, I'll save at least $500 a month and you can help me take care of the kids every other weekend," he stated as he continued to survey his surroundings like a king looking out at his glorious lands.

Speechless. I was speechless. Say something for God's

sake, I told myself. Cough or choke or force a fart … make some kind of noise so that he breaks out of that stupid trance and we can return to reality! Don't let him believe that you are thinking about it, actually considering this madman's suggestion. Isn't silence often mistaken for acceptance? What? Get $500 compensation per month to have this man move his crap into my beautiful house, put up with his maniacal moods and over the top O.C.D.-ness every single day? Oh, and let's not forget the added bonus of getting to spend quality time with the two pouting pre-teens who love my company so much. Egad. I wondered if I should laugh out loud, or would that have been rude?

"Ha ha," I managed a pathetic little laugh. "I don't think so, mister." Case closed.

George continued with his attempt to convince me of how it was such a good deal (for him, of course) to move in with me over the next several months. This, combined with his habit of vacuuming my chairs and couch every time he came to visit, helped me to quickly determine that he was not to be considered a candidate for long-term companionship. Yes, I said he vacuumed my furniture. Why? Because there was dog hair all over them. Every time he sat on the couch or one of the chairs, he would jump back up and frantically wipe the hair off his clothes while making disgusted grunting noises loud enough for me to hear. He would then go get my vacuum cleaner out of the closet and proceed to remove all the dog hair from all of my furniture. He would rant and rave about how the dog shouldn't be up on the furniture getting dog hair all over it. Yes, you know what I told him, I know you saw this one coming.

"George, the dog lives here. You don't. Get over it or don't sit on the furniture," I told him.

On a good note, I was very happy to have George vacuum my furniture every time he visited! What was even more entertaining was when we would sit on the couch together, and I would coax the dog to get up on the furniture – between us. George was close to having a coronary several times.

Yes, things began to unravel quickly at that point. The last straw with George was when he gave me a frying pan for Christmas because mine was scratched and old. A frying pan! Oh, you know how we women just love to get frying pans or blenders or other assorted household items as Christmas gifts. Funny thing, though. I still have that frying pan almost 15 years later, and my current dog gets to lie on all the furniture.

In the end, when I told George that I didn't see a future for us together, he said he was very disappointed, as he had been planning to ask me to marry him. Poor guy. I replied in pure Rose fashion, "I'm sure glad you didn't. You would have gotten your feelings seriously hurt." That poor man was absolutely serious! I believe George was simply looking for someone to make his life easier and wasn't necessarily interested in finding his perfect mate.

George called me several years later and shared with me that he was going through a divorce. After our chapter ended, George met a woman online who owned a home and had several children of her own. They married, he moved in, and while there may have been harmony at first, it soon ended. The harsh reality of rushing into a relationship for the wrong reasons and trying to create a harmonious family situation didn't last long. He explained that she was crazy, her children were unbearable and he simply had to get out. Unfortunately, part of that problem was George, who may not have been looking for the right person for the right reason. It's not enough to just want to be in a relationship or be married. There are many other factors that play into being the right package for the right person.

Another Frog I kissed just a few months shortly before meeting my Prince Charming was similar to George in the fact that he wanted something specific from me. And just the mere fact that he would come out and actually ask me for it was enough to cause me to throw him back into the dating pond. I didn't immediately realize what his ultimate intentions were, but, like George, there were small things that didn't gel between us.

Ron was a big guy, a real man's man. I'm not a little girl, but he made me feel like one. He must have been about 6'3" with big broad shoulders. I liked the look of his photos and he had an awesome smile. After a few evening chats on the phone, we decided to meet on a Saturday night at The Cheesecake Factory. Ron picked the location, as it was located approximately halfway between where we both lived, which made it convenient. Wait. Before I continue with Ron, let me share another very important factor about meeting men who you don't know.

One of my greatest fears in life is my personal safety – always has been and still is today, I must admit. You wouldn't think I would be willing to go on so many blind dates if this were the case; however, I always made sure I did one important thing. Before going on every first date, I would call, text or email one of my sisters or girlfriends with the following information: my date's profile name and which website he was on, his real name (or what he said it was), his phone number, and where and when we were meeting for our date. This is vitally important and while it may seem overly cautious, I can't over emphasize the importance of being safe. Do not believe that every word you are told is the absolute truth. Always let someone know where you will be, who you will be with, and then check in after the date is over. During especially successful dates that may have lasted longer than my sister or girlfriend thought they should, I would always get a text or call at a certain point during the date asking if I was okay. This made me feel safe and is exactly how it should be. Please consider letting someone be your safety net and incorporating this practice if you go on a blind date. Now, back to Ron.

Meeting Ron was easy and fun. I liked his look as soon as I saw him standing in front of the restaurant and enjoyed the bear hug from this big hunk of a manly man. After we were seated, he shared with me that he lived in a certain upscale neighborhood down south, he drove a gold Mercedes convertible and he had been in the military. He owned a small carpet cleaning business and lived near his ex-wife. He didn't speak ill of her at all and said he saw his sons every day after they got out of school. This sounded like a man who had his life in order. I was impressed and interested.

The dinner went very well and we both ate the same thing. We had a drink, ate our dinner and split a yummy piece of cheesecake. The conversation was easy; he asked questions of me and seemed interested in what I had to say. He paid for the dinner, although I offered to pay for my own. He was a true gentleman in every sense of the word.

I offered to treat him to dinner at a little Mexican place near my home the following weekend. Date two was set and it appeared all was going well. We said goodbye at the front door of the restaurant and I considered it a successful first date. And then, of course, I called my sister.

Ron arrived at my house the following weekend and I was excited to get to know this man better. He came to the door of my house, I invited him in for a moment (but didn't give him the grand tour like I did with George), and off we went on our date.

As we stepped out onto the driveway, Ron asked if I would mind driving to dinner rather than us going in his car. His car – the gold Mercedes convertible, remember? Well, yes, it was a gold Mercedes convertible but Ron hadn't shared with me that it was about 30 years old and needed some serious work. Rips in the top of the convertible canopy, missing molding, and the inside was in extreme disrepair.

I didn't care what his car looked like. Let me be clear about that. And I didn't mind driving us to dinner in my very clean, extremely well kept car. What I did mind, however, was finding out that his gold Mercedes convertible had a very bad oil leak and while we were at dinner, it did a very good job of doing just that on my clean driveway. I am a perfectionist, and that flows out into my yard, my sidewalks and my driveway. I once spent a solid weekend power washing my driveway. Yes, I'm a freak, but I can live with that fact. What I couldn't live with was Ron's car leaking oil all over my clean driveway while we were eating Mexican food.

Naturally, I didn't see this oil spot until he drove away after returning to my house. But let me ask you this. If you know that your car leaks oil very badly (because yes, you have to keep adding oil to it or the engine will freeze up and leave you stranded), wouldn't you park on the street instead of in someone's driveway? I certainly would, but I doubt I would drive a car that leaked oil in the first place, so never mind. I actually never had the opportunity to mention it to Ron, though, as he never returned to my house again. It appeared that the leaking oil situation wasn't the only issue Ron was experiencing.

I found out during our second dinner together that Ron lived in a one-bedroom apartment right next to (not in) the upscale neighborhood that his wife lived in. She'd kept the house during the divorce and he had moved into an apartment. Nothing wrong with that, but it helped put things in perspective when he shared with me what he ultimately wanted.

The following week, Ron called me to say hello. I was relaxing by laying on the couch after a long day at work. I was trying to decide if I wanted to go take a quick walk before it got dark outside.

"I have something to ask you," Ron said. "Please give it some thought. This is very hard for me to do."

This certainly got my attention, and I sat up straight on the couch.

"If I had anyone else I could ask," Ron continued, "I

would. But I don't."

I was all ears. I sure hoped he wasn't going to ask me to donate a kidney, because I'd gotten rather attached to both of mine over the years. I probably would have taken that request more easily than his actual request. What he did want spoke unfavorably of his true character, in my opinion. Very loudly, actually.

Ron continued that he was in a tough spot and needed my help. He understood if I couldn't help him out, but he really needed to ask.

I sat there on my couch anxiously anticipating having to consider which kidney to part with.

"I desperately need to borrow $300. I can pay you back on Friday, but I really need your help. I will definitely pay you back, I promise. It's just very important that I get the $300 tonight. Would you be able to help me?" Ron asked.

I was speechless while at the same time thankful that both of my beloved kidneys were safe.

"Did you seriously just ask to borrow $300 from me, Ron?" I said.

"I hate to have to do it, but I'm in a very tight spot. Would you please consider helping me out?" Ron continued.

Now, here I was, realizing that this man needed something from me that he truly shouldn't have been asking for from a woman he had just met 10 days ago. Didn't he have anyone else in his life that he could ask? A family member, a friend, his ex-wife? But no, he chose to ask me for $300. And to me, it was about anything but the $300.

"I am in shock, Ron," I said. "I'm speechless. Somehow you think its okay to ask me for money. We've known each other for less than two weeks and I can't believe there isn't someone else in your life who you can ask for a loan."

I went on to explain that it wasn't about the amount of his request; it was that he thought it was acceptable to even ask me. The truth was that, financially, I could have given him ten times that amount with no problem. However, the hard fact was that this man shouldn't have been asking me for a loan for any amount when we'd only known each other 10 days.

"Ron," I continued, "this says a lot about the type of man you are. If you truly think it's acceptable to ask me for a loan, I certainly gave you more credit than you deserve. It's not that I can't give you the loan, it's that I won't give you the loan. It has nothing to do with the money and everything to do with the man you aren't."

With that, Ron thanked me and hung up the phone. I never heard from him again.

The point of these stories is that it's important to want to be with someone for the right reasons. Relationships should bring good from and in to both sides. It's not a one-sided proposition. If one person has a lot of baggage and the other person has none, there is a great probability that there will be future issues.

If you meet someone who wants to change you from the beginning, let them go. If you find a nice guy, but as you sit across the table from him at dinner, you find yourself disgusted by the way he chews and talks with his mouth full of food, then guess what? You won't be able to change that about him. Nagging him about it in the future will only decrease the favorable emotions you might now share. In that sense, you may meet someone and during the first dinner date, you say something clever and because he chews with his mouth open, he may laugh and spit a wad of his food across the table to land directly on your cheek. No, just not pretty. Let him go.

If you meet a nice lady online and like her, but she complains constantly about how she was screwed over by her cheating ex-husband and tells how she plans to make his life a living hell, run the other way. You will forever be a part of that person's drama. If he drinks too much or she has a potty mouth, that's who they are. It doesn't change. And you aren't going to be the person to change them.

Who you meet initially online or in any dating situation is exactly what you get. It's a pre-packaged deal, remember. It comes simply and precisely the way you see it sitting on the shelf. Whatever beliefs, morals or standards they have will be constant throughout the entire time you know them. If you accept this fact and preset your standards of what is acceptable or not acceptable before you meet anyone, and then choose to not settle, you will eventually find that special person. There is no such thing as too picky when it comes down to personal standards and desires. But you have to be willing to spend some time alone and, yes, that means life may be tougher for a while – emotionally, financially and physically. However, it will be worth it in the end. I kissed Frogs for nine years before I found my Prince Charming. He or she is out there for you, too. It may just take a lot more Chapstick or lip balm than you initially anticipated. Stock up, sister. 🐸

DON'T BE AFRAID TO PUT YOURSELF FIRST – ALWAYS BE TRUE TO YOU

I have to admit that as I've shared some of my stories about my online dating experiences with friends, both male and female, they often exclaim that they can't believe I said or did some of things that I have in different dating situations. That puzzles me, as I only know how to be me. In doing so, I believe that we should all be true to ourselves, make the decisions that align with what we want or can accept and put those personal values first. Yes, that means in some cases a choice will have to be made that may seem harsh or mean. Feelings may be hurt at the moment, but in the long run, making the hard decision can eliminate a lot of personal grief and cut short what is surely a bad situation.

I learned early on that I needed to be true to myself in every aspect. It would do no good to me or my potential Prince if I changed to be someone I wasn't. That meant knowing up front what I wanted and would or would not accept in a mate. For instance, take Jeff, who I met at a park in our town on a nice Saturday morning to see if we were compatible. We had fun chatting online and after a few weeks, decided to meet. I hadn't had much luck yet with the other Frogs I had met and didn't really hold out much hope that Jeff would be different.

When I showed up at the park, Jeff was already sitting at a picnic table waiting for me. I introduced myself to him and sat directly across the table from him. In looking at Jeff closely, he had an eerie resemblance to my ex-husband that

I hadn't keyed in on from his profile photos. I mean, they could have been brothers if not almost twins. The same curly hair, the same facial features, the same build and even the same hands. It was kind of freaky in every way. I didn't think that I could consider dating Jeff, as I would surely always be thinking of my ex-husband who put me in this situation of having to kiss Frogs in the first place. And then I noticed something odd about Jeff. Every time he spoke to me, he covered up his mouth with his hand or put his head down and stared down at the table. What the heck? I was super curious and was determined to figure out what he was hiding. Unfortunately, I wasn't happy when I discovered what it was.

Jeff was certainly nice enough, but what was the deal with him hiding his mouth? I kept sneaking peeks and finally turned to outright staring in an attempt to discover his secret. Eventually it revealed itself. Jeff was in desperate need of a cosmetic dentist, and I mean seriously. I made him laugh at one point and he threw his head back, opened up his mouth and revealed a mouthful of rotten teeth. And when I say rotten, I mean some of them were absolutely black. There were a few missing as well. It was not pretty. This was one Frog I would absolutely not be kissing at all. The words of my girlfriend came rushing into my head. Whenever we would see a guy with the need for dentistry, she would put one of her long, manicured fingernails over her front tooth and say, "Snaggle tooth. Get your teef fixed!"

I didn't have another date with Jeff, although he emailed me and wanted to meet again. I did share with him that he was eerily similar to my ex-husband in way too many ways for words. However, I did not share with him that his mouth full of rotten teeth was simply disgusting. There was no need to be cruel, and even if he had a straight, white set of choppers, I would not have been able to date him. There just would have been too many memories that would have freaked me out when I looked at him. So, being true to me, I had to let him go.

Another Frog I met had to be thrown back into the pond fairly quickly as I simply didn't feel I was a priority to him. His name was Carlton and I was quite enamored with the fact that he was a DPS Trooper. You know how we women love a man in uniform! What a respectable job to have, and I was impressed after meeting him the first time. We got along well on our first date at a little place downtown one weeknight. We ate and had a beer, enjoyed each other's company and shared about our backgrounds, experiences and previous military careers. I felt very comfortable with Carlton so I had no qualms about accepting his offer to cook me dinner at his place that upcoming weekend. After all, he was an officer of the law, so I didn't really have any issues with going to his home. Besides, my girlfriend would know where I was and whom I was with.

On the following Saturday evening, I showed up at Carlton's apartment carrying a bottle of wine and was anxious for the date. He answered my knock on the door and apologized that he was running behind on preparing dinner. He had planned to bake fish with a new recipe but was still in the middle of preparing it. I didn't mind, I said, and sat on the couch watching him make dinner while drinking wine and making conversation. Our date was at 7 p.m. and I believe it was 8:45 p.m. when we finally sat down at his table to enjoy the baked fish he prepared. Conversation was casual, dinner was good and the company was great – well, at least that's what I thought.

After the dishes were cleaned up, Carlton asked me if I would like to stay and watch a movie. Although it was 9:30 at night, I didn't have anywhere else to go and was enjoying being with him. We agreed on the movie to watch and got comfortable on his couch. Now first let me explain how Carlton's apartment was set up. His couch was on a long wall that faced the small kitchen and dining room. His TV was at the far end of the couch to the left on the other side of the front door. If you walked into his apartment through the front door, the couch would be directly to your right along the wall while the TV would be directly to your left on the other side of the door. There were no other chairs or places to sit in that room. Watching a movie together meant that one of us would likely have to look around the head of the other person. But Carlton had a better idea.

He positioned me sitting up at the far end of the couch furthest away from the TV with a pillow in my lap. Then he proceeded to lie down on the couch and put his head in my lap. Oh, you think, how very romantic. Guess again. He must have had such a great view above him from his vantage point lying on my lap … of the inside of my nostrils and the loose skin under my chin.

It wouldn't have been so bad if he would have stayed awake long enough to enjoy that not so perfect view. But, no. Within two minutes of the movie starting, Carlton had not only fallen asleep but was snoring. Loudly. So there I sat, providing comfort and warmth to this man who would rather fall asleep while watching a movie than sit up and attack me like a hot blooded man should. Didn't it make sense that he would want to at least kiss me and try to make out with me? Shouldn't he have been trying to pull me out of the living room into the only other room in the apartment – his bedroom? Regardless of whether I would resist or not. But, no. He slept and I watched the movie.

Carlton not only slept through the movie, he also appeared to have gone into a slight coma. No manner of my moving roused this man. I moved my legs that had long since gone to sleep and turned to concrete, to no avail. He continued to snore and dream peacefully.

After the movie ended, I pushed Carlton's head off my lap and placed his head on the couch. Yes, you guessed it. He was still sound asleep. I wasn't feeling the love at that moment, and in all actuality, I wasn't even feeling the like. It was time for me to remove myself from the sad situation. Did I try harder to wake him up or did I just leave? I stood next to the couch looking down at Carlton sleeping like a baby, completely unaware that I was standing over him or even that I was still in his apartment.

What would he say if I had actually been able to wake him up? Would it matter or impact how insignificant I was feeling at that moment? No. It wouldn't. My mind was made up. I walked over to the counter, picked up my purse and headed towards the door. I paused for a moment and wondered if I should leave him a note. Nope. Not necessary. I'd write him an email when I got back to my house. Opening the door, I slipped out into the crisp night air and walked unescorted to my car.

I called my girlfriend who was waiting to hear from me and let her know how the night went. Not the best ending to an evening, but I felt very good about how I remained true to myself and made the decision to leave. I deserved better than spending the night with someone who would rather sleep. I sent Carlton an email when I got back to my house wherein I basically told him that I deserved better than the evening he served up. He didn't reply.

Another evening that ended oddly and took me by surprise was my first date with Ned. After great conversation online and a few interesting phone calls, we agreed to meet for dinner Saturday at a Mexican restaurant at the mall. Ned had a great sense of humor and I enjoyed the date as we laughed over margaritas and ate dinner. He was attractive, charming and very easy to be around. We ordered our second margarita and Ned asked me a very odd question.

"Do you want to go buy a sexy negligee at Victoria's Secret, Rose?" he said as he took a long drink from his frozen margarita.

"What? Are you serious?" I said to him. "Why would we do that?" I think I may have blushed.

Ned explained that there was just something erotic about buying women sexy negligees. He loved that store and it would make him very happy if I agreed to at least walk down there with him. Since I had just finished my second margarita and needed to let some of the alcohol buzz wear off before driving back home, I agreed.

We walked together down to Victoria's Secret in the mall. It felt very odd as I walked along with this stranger who wanted to buy me a negligee. I wondered if Ned thought he would get to watch me try it on. That wouldn't happen in this girl's lifetime. I did let him choose the negligee since he planned to pay for it. Ned took his time as he walked around the store and looked at the many options. He touched so many of the lacy, sexy choices and finally held up a two-piece negligee and asked me what I thought.

"It is fine, Ned," I replied without much conviction, "But I don't believe it's necessary to spend that much money on a pair of pajamas that will not be comfortable and are only designed to end up on the floor." Ned laughed.

I was being true to myself in only one aspect, as I had no intention to ever wear the negligee. I gave him an out to save his money. He refused, held the negligee out to me and off I trudged to the dressing room. I heard Ned call after me, "Will you come out and show me how it fits?" I ignored him.

Ned appeared to have lost his mind as I had no intention to show him how the sexy outfit fit at that point or any time in the future. Had there been a back exit out of the store or dressing room, I would have been able to sneak out undetected. My main thought was how many women had he taken to dinner and shopping at this mall who agreed to let him see how the negligee fit. I agreed to this charade and I had to get myself out of it.

As I came out of the dressing room, Ned asked how the negligee fit. I told him, "Just perfect." With that, he paid too much money for it and handed me the fancy pink and black bag. We walked out the mall doors by the restaurant, I thanked him for a great evening and drove home. I was not happy with my decision to feel pressured into letting Ned buy me a negligee. I should have said no. My being true to myself did not include shopping at Victoria's Secret on a first date.

That negligee never made it out of that fancy pink and black bag after I immediately put it on the top shelf of my closet. I couldn't bring myself to ever try it on again. Years later I gave it to a girlfriend who hopefully put it to good use. As for Ned, I refused his calls and promised myself to stay true to my values. I would not be pressured to do something that didn't feel right on another first date.

My most memorable experience with this particular lesson of remaining true to myself begins with Fred from Dallas. Now, typically I wouldn't have entertained the idea of seeing someone from another city; however, I was at the point in my online dating career (it seemed like a job sometimes) where I was becoming bored of the local fare. I thought perhaps I could meet someone from further away who I wouldn't see very much but may still enjoy getting to know.

Fred was a Lt. Colonel in the Air Force Reserves, which was appealing as I was recently retired from the Air Force. He messaged me first, as I wasn't actively searching for guys outside the local area, and we chatted online for about a week. Shortly thereafter we began having phone conversations, which were positive, uplifting and fun. (This part would come back to haunt us later in my story. It didn't remain quite so positive and uplifting, to say the very least.)

At the end of that first week of phone conversations, Fred suggested that he come to visit me the upcoming weekend. He said he'd fly down to Austin and we could spend the weekend getting to know each other, take in some sites and maybe go see a baseball game together. I thought, 'Well, why the heck not?' He seemed like a really nice guy. He was a military career man and it might be nice to spend some time with him. I thought he was attractive but, again, this was based solely on the pictures he posted on his profile, which I still remember clearly. One photo was his military portrait in full uniform with head gear, and the other more appealing one was of him standing next to a red corvette in jeans and a T-shirt with a bandana tied around his head.

So I agreed – yes, let's meet. Fred made plans to come see me the following weekend. He would fly in on Friday evening and leave on Sunday. I felt so good about our connection that I even offered to let him stay at my house in my guest room. Why spend the money on a hotel when I had the extra room?

"What? Have you lost your mind? Are you crazy? He could be a serial killer!" fussed my sister Liz.

My teenage son would be with me that weekend, and although he'd be out hanging with his friends, at least he would be home at night, right? Little did I know at that time that we would never even get that far into this story of our weekend together.

The day arrived with excitement and anticipation. I rushed home from work, freshened up a little (a girl wants to make a good first impression, right?) and off I went to the airport to pick up Fred. How exciting it is to meet someone for the first time! All those great email exchanges and phone conversations will culminate in a face-to-face meeting with perhaps a spark or two.

I got to the airport early so I could go inside and meet Fred at the baggage claim area. I knew he would recognize me right away, as I was adamant about putting very recent, accurate and honest photos on my dating profile. It helped that I had a multi-colored, unique hairstyle that was hard to hide or imitate! It also helped that I posted roughly 12 photos on my profile, unlike only two from Fred. I only hoped that I would recognize Fred as easily as he would me.

So there I was, standing in baggage claim with butterflies in my stomach and sweaty palms, watching the assortment of guys coming down the escalator on this Friday night. A nice looking man stepped onto the top of the escalator. Was that him? Was he looking around for me? No, not Fred, and that wedding ring on the man's hand would have been an issue. Oh, wow. A very attractive guy came down the escalator. Was it him? Please let that guy be him, I thought. Please let that be him! Nope. Not him. Didn't look anything like him, actually.

I checked the monitor for arrivals. Fred's plane had landed, and he would be coming down the escalator at any moment. Perhaps he would come down the other escalator on the left side of the baggage claim. 'Should I walk over there?' I wondered. 'Will I miss seeing him approach? What if he walks right by me?'

Wait. Oh no. Who was that man at the top of the escalator? (My heart sank, and my butterflies turned to cement and fell straight to my colon.) Seriously? Was that him? No, it couldn't be. How had I missed that? There was something not quite right about Fred. Or more specifically, Fred's hair. How had I flipping missed that?

Could I blend back into the crowd? Could I run for dear life? Slip away to the bathroom, perhaps? Had he seen me? All these thoughts flashed through my mind in a millisecond, but then it happened. Oh dear God. That same man smiled and waved at me. Yup. It was Fred.

This Fred, in all his glory inching closer to my spot in the baggage claim area, was not the Fred of my imagination or dreams. It was also not the Fred of his online dating profile either, was it? This Fred was wearing white knee-high socks with black tennis shoes, unflattering too-short blue gym shorts and a government issued gray T-shirt with US AIR FORCE stamped across the chest. He wasn't bad looking, but he had absolutely no sense of style. Nice smile, yes. But that hair... or should I say hairpiece. A hairpiece, a toupee! I'd been duped! I'd been tricked! I'd been bamboozled! I had about five seconds before Fred stepped off the escalator. It was too late to run.

I closed my eyes and said a quick but heartfelt and sincere prayer: 'Oh dear Lord, please hear me now. Help me disappear. I need your promised rapture right now! Please let your beloved son Jesus appear to the world at this very moment so all that is left of me are my clothes lying on the airport floor in front of this approaching man. Please hear my prayer and deliver me to your divine presence. In your Holy Son's name, Amen.' I opened one of my eyes – was I in heaven?

Oh crap. I was still there at the airport and there was Fred, stepping off the escalator and bouncing towards me.

How had I missed that one little point? I don't like toupees! I detest toupees! My sisters and I used to play a game when we went anywhere together. If one of us saw a guy in a bad toupee (and most toupees are bad), we'd say out loud, "Toop alert," and the others would have to identify the guy. Besides the unfortunate fact that I'd had one date with a guy who decided to kiss me at the end of the evening on a first date, so, wanting to be friendly and kiss him back, my hand went to the back of his neck where my fingers slipped right under the rubber of his full toupee! Both of our eyes popped open, he was mortified and I almost puked in my mouth (and his). Not a good experience for either of us at all. There was no second date; however, his toupee was better than most – minus my fingers trying to dislodge it from his head.

Well crap and crap again. Back to Fred and his poor sense of style and even less stylish toupee. I had the urge to yell "Toop alert" and run out the door, but that wasn't happening. I was going to have to put on my big girl panties, keep my fingers off his head and face the music. 'At least he's a nice guy with a great personality and we have a sincere connection,' I told myself. Think again and keep reading.

"Hi, Rose! You look just like your pictures but you're even prettier! I could have recognized you out of a hundred girls standing here," came the last positive words of the night from Fred, the toupee wearing, badly dressed visitor from Dallas.

I returned the hello but not the compliment. No wonder he'd had his hat on in his military photo and had the bandana tied around his head. I should always go with my intuition. I had thought there was something not quite right about those photos but, hey, I sound very shallow right now. Looks are only part of the package and if this had been the only issue, it may have been a great weekend. No attraction on my part, but it still could have been a great time spent together … if only the story stopped here. Unfortunately I'm just getting started.

Read on please.

Out to my car we walked after leaving baggage claim, and that's when bad turned ugly. Fred started complaining. About everything. The flight was bumpy and he'd had to sit by a lady with a screaming child. The refreshments on the plane sucked and there was no legroom. As we left the airport in my car and got on the freeway, Fred was still vomiting out his negativity.

"The traffic sucks tonight," he complained. Then he started on his ex-wife, how he hated her and wished a big truck would hit her. He went on about his enormous alimony payments, how he had to sell the red Corvette just to pay his attorney. How she cheated on him and was now living happily with her new man.

Oh, wow. I hadn't seen all that coming down the escalator with that fake hair. Where was this man when we had spoken on the phone the week before? Phone-Fred had been so positive, asking leading questions, talking about his job and how much he loved the Air Force. The real Fred, sitting next to me in my car as we got closer and closer to my house, wouldn't shut up and every word he spewed from his mouth was a negative, nasty, mean spirited comment. Everything was someone else's fault. He was the helpless, hopeless victim.

I panicked! I couldn't take this man to my house! I couldn't let him know where I lived. What would I do? He was supposed to stay at my house for the next two nights, and I had planned to waltz him around my community like someone I wanted to be seen with. Except I didn't want to be seen with him!

I exited from the freeway near my home and I needed to make a decision. Once I turned left at the light, I would be committed to taking him to my house. So, I instead took a right at the light and we headed away from my neighborhood. What to do? Where to go?! I continued towards a little hole in the wall Mexican restaurant where I was certain no one I knew would be on that Friday night from hell.

"Let's have dinner, shall we?" I said as I interrupted his complaints. I pulled up to the restaurant, parked and jumped out as fast as I could.

As we walked into the restaurant, Fred continued to berate his ex-wife and spout off all her faults.

I needed to think and I needed a strong margarita – badly. My mind was reeling. I felt trapped. This was much more than a "Calgon, take me away" moment!

We sat down at the table, ordered our drinks and stared at the menu.

How could I spend two days listening to that man? What in the world would I do? What in tarnation was I thinking when I agreed to this plan? How could I have been so stupid? I didn't want anyone to see me with that negative specimen of an unhappy human being sans toupee. We couldn't hide in my house the whole weekend. I didn't even want my son to be around him. I couldn't do it. I simply couldn't do it. I. Couldn't. Do. It!

"You can't do what? Order dinner?" said Fred as he looked up from the menu across the table from me.

Oh holy crap. Had I said that out loud? I had! I'd said that sentence out loud and Fred had heard me. Holy crap again, now what would I do? Well, I was committed then. It was time to be true to myself. "No, I can't do this," I said. "I can't spend the weekend with you, Fred."

Needless to say, Fred was shocked, insulted and not very happy. But it wasn't much of a difference from the negative Fred of three minutes before. I had to explain to him that he wasn't who I'd thought he was. I didn't like how negative he was about everything and I was quite surprised by how ugly he'd been about his past relationship. We were not compatible after all and I didn't want to invite him to my home for the weekend. I didn't want to spend time with him. I just couldn't do it.

"What am I supposed to do now then?" Fred asked. "The last flight on Southwest returns to Dallas in less than a half hour. Where am I supposed to go?" Fred whined and complained while I continued to eat. He then realized I was serious. "If I can get on a flight tomorrow morning, can I at least stay at your house tonight?" he asked.

What would you have done at that point? Taken him to your house, invited that ugliness into your positive environment and subjected your son to some of that nonsense? No. I told Fred that he would need to get a hotel near the airport and that I'd be happy to drive him back there that night.

And that is exactly what we did. He called Southwest Airlines, changed his flight from Sunday afternoon to Saturday morning, and paid his flight change fee.

As Fred continued to show his ugliness, my heart lifted and my stress released. I was almost euphoric! We finished dinner in near-silence with the only words spoken being more complaints from my soon to be ex-weekend date. Fred couldn't help himself. After all, I'd given him a whole new experience to complain about.

We left the restaurant and I felt like I was walking on air. I was going to be rid of that negative, unsavory specimen of a Frog! I drove him back to the hotel of his choice near the airport, said goodbye, and drove away as Fred mumbled about the expense of the changed flight and room charge. But, hey, at least I paid for dinner.

I did the right thing with Fred. I cut my losses and set him free. He wasn't compatible with me in the end and there was no reason to delay the inevitable. Had I spent the weekend with him, I wouldn't have been true to myself. I would have settled, even if only for a weekend. I would have hated every moment of it, and I knew it would be best to take a stand albeit uncomfortable for us both. It was harsh, but I had been honest and painfully open, and I don't regret having done so.

I received one final email from Fred on Sunday evening. It wasn't very nice, and perhaps some of it was well deserved. But did I regret taking a stand and being true to myself? Not for one moment. And no, I did not reply to Fred's email. Delete, delete, delete.

Fred's version of this story about our meeting would be written differently, but this isn't his story, is it? Fred probably wouldn't encourage you to do the right thing for yourself. But I'm telling you this: Always listen to your intuition and be true to yourself. You have 24 hours in each day. You are in complete control of how you get to spend those precious hours and in whom you invest that time. Perhaps you are spending time right now with someone you absolutely know in your heart is not the person for you. What are you waiting for? Don't delay. Be picky. Make the best choice for yourself. Do the right thing. You absolutely deserve it. ⟫

ALWAYS LISTEN TO YOUR
INTUITION – SHE ISN'T
JUST THAT BITCH
INSIDE YOUR HEAD

It's easy to talk yourself into something even when the voice of intuition inside your head is screaming loudly. I believe this is especially true when participating in online dating. We online daters would prefer for things to go down a certain path and want so desperately to have the merry-go-round of electronic winks, playful texts, endless emails and phone conversations, followed by the disappointing dates to simply stop. Perhaps you or someone you know didn't have to spend the better part of nine years of their single life exploring possibilities on various dating websites and riding the dating merry-go-round. I do know a few lucky ones who actually kissed only one or two Frogs and immediately met their Prince Charming or Princess in a very short time period. I wasn't that fortunate, and the great majority of those millions of participants with active online profiles usually are not that lucky, either. I'm not trying to dissuade anyone from trying internet dating. On the contrary! I am 100 percent in favor of the opportunity; however, I would be more content if those engaging in this activity would follow common sense etiquette. But as much as I'd like to blame the other person, there were a few Frogs I kissed that would have never entered my life had I listened to my intuition. The fact of the matter is this: When I do listen to that sometimes-screaming voice having a particularly ugly childish hissy fit in my head, I am always thankful that I did. However, the following are not examples of those instances of clarity or rationale.

The very first time I heard that voice in my head on a date was when I went to meet Sal. He had the most interesting photos on his profile and I was quite intrigued. Sal was an American Indian, (feathers … not dot) and his pictures spotlighted that fact. In his main profile photo, he wore a full headdress, was bare-chested, and wore some type of animal skins on his legs. He was standing on a huge rock (the photo was taken from an angle below him) and he was holding a bow and arrow in his hands. He had jet-black long hair and, yes, it was in braids. Extremely interesting indeed. Another photo showed him playing some type of wooden instrument – not exactly a flute, but similar to that, except he held it down in front of him like a clarinet. I liked the idea that he was very comfortable showing his heritage. We wrote to each other for a few weeks and then he asked me to come meet him near his home.

Sal and I agreed to meet at a local coffee shop on a Friday evening, and when I showed up he was waiting inside for me. He still had a lot of hair, although it wasn't quite as long as it had been in his photos. He wore tinted glasses and a black leather jacket.

We ordered our drinks (coffee for him and Diet Coke for me) and sat at a table near the window. We passed an hour with small talk and questions about each other. He seemed quite interested in me but I wasn't quite sure what I thought about him. I found it strange that he wouldn't take off his tinted glasses – I wasn't sure if they were sunglasses or regular glasses, but since it was dark outside, it seemed unnecessary to be wearing them.

When we were finished with our drinks, Sal asked if I wanted to come over to his house to listen to his music that he recorded of himself playing that Native American instrument. We were walking out towards my car, and it was at that point that the voice in my head started screaming her head off. You don't know this man! No one knows you are going to his house! You don't even know his address! What are you doing?!

"Come over for just a few minutes," Sal pleaded as I stood next to my car. "You can leave whenever you want." He seemed sincere and harmless.

With the crazy lady screaming inside my head, I agreed to come over for just a little bit, even at my own inner hesitancy. He asked me to follow him to his house around the corner and down the block. I was not feeling good about this and should have left right then.

When we pulled up in front of Sal's house, I stayed inside my car. It had started to rain, which I should have taken as a sign. I actually sat there long enough for Sal to come over and tap on my window. I simply didn't feel good about getting out of my car. Again, Sal repeated that I could leave whenever I wanted to. Against my better judgment, I opened my car door and got out. My voice of intuition was screaming so loudly that I couldn't even think straight. This was not a wise decision I had just made.

Sal and I ran to his front porch and he let me inside his small but tidy house. It was an older house and looked like he was doing some remodeling. He offered me a beer and a hand towel to wipe off the rain. I accepted the towel but declined having a beer. I needed to keep my wits sharp and not be influenced by alcohol. I knew I had no right to be inside that house with that strange man. No one knew where I was once I had left the coffee shop. This was not a smart move and the bitch in my head agreed wholeheartedly about that point.

I tried to look interested when Sal showed me his photos on the wall. It appeared he was into photography, which explained why he had such interesting pictures on his dating profile. He gave me the tour of his small two-bedroom home and asked if I'd like to hear him play his flute-like instrument. I said I would and he proceeded to play a haunting tune that had a way of cutting right through to my bones. He was still wearing his tinted glasses but as he finished playing his song, he removed them.

Although Sal tried to avoid looking directly at me, I now knew why he wore the tinted glasses. His left eye was either lazy or he had been injured as it did not look in the same direction that his right eye did. He was still an attractive man, but I was just not feeling comfortable alone in his house.

Sal came up to me after taking off his glasses and took me in his arms and kissed me. He was quite insistent in his kiss and tried to push me towards his guest bedroom.

That voice in my head was doing her absolute best to tell me to get the hell out of that house. "And I mean right now and in a hurry!" she screamed. I had to agree with her. I simply shouldn't have been there and I should have listened to her when we had left the coffee shop. I had put myself in a very precarious position. How would I get out of this mess? Honesty. Tell Sal exactly how I felt. And hope to God he was a nice guy and not a raving lunatic hell bent on making me his right there and then. Lord help me if he had plans worse than that!

I explained to Sal that I shouldn't be there. We didn't know each other and while I appreciated his invitation, I needed to go. My sister expected me to call her and I was already late in doing that. I thanked him for the nice evening and started walking towards the front door.

Sal stepped in front of me when I got to the door and again took me in his arms. "I don't want you to go," he said. "I'm lonely. Will you please stay?"

I was feeling quite nervous then and knew I had made a grave error in ever agreeing to come to Sal's house. I should have known better! Why hadn't I listened to my intuition and done what I knew was the right thing? I reached for the front door and told Sal, "I really have to go, but I'll call you tomorrow. Thank you for the nice evening." I walked out of the house, down the sidewalk and simply couldn't get in my car fast enough.

Sal didn't follow me and didn't even wait until I got in the car to shut the door. He was gone from sight.

As soon as I got in my car, I called my sister. When I told her what I'd done, she was furious and had every right to be. This behavior went completely against my grain and I knew better! She scolded me and I agreed with her. This could have turned out so very badly. I promised her that I would never go to a man's house again on a first date, and I kept that promise.

You can't be too careful, and I should have listened to my intuition the minute Sal suggested we go to his house. I could have easily made the excuse that I needed to go somewhere else. It became apparent to me that he had planned our date so close to his house as it had been his intention to ask me over to his house. I'm certain he had hopes for more intimacy than he got that night, and I made the decision to not call him the following day or have anything further to do with him. He never attempted to contact me, either.

Any man who would put a woman in such a compromising position on the first date clearly has more intentions than he should. It wasn't Sal's fault in the long run. He made a suggestion and I agreed to go. Luckily, I was able to remove myself safely from the situation and learned a valuable lesson. My intuition is a loud, strong voice. I needed to listen to her. While I may not have always listened to her immediately, eventually she got my full attention in all cases in the future. Let me share a few more.

When I started communicating with Rick, I was at that phase of my internet dating experience where I was using dating websites as entertainment rather than truly trying to meet someone. I wasn't committed to finding my Prince Charming as I wasn't certain he even existed or if I even wanted him to. I was enjoying the attention and mainly used the emails and text feature on the websites as time killers. I quickly blocked those members who had the audacity to ask me if I was even interested in meeting them or if I was just playing games. 'Huh? Playing games? How rude to even suggest that I would do such a thing,' I thought. And then the little voice in the back of my head, my know-it-all intuition, spoke up – and not for the last time –

to suggest that those guys were right. I really didn't want to leave the safety of my little office tucked upstairs inside my quaint little home to venture out to meet and possibly kiss any of these particular Frogs. I'd already had enough unsatisfactory, bad experiences in the dating pond. Why not spend the time as a safe observer on the side of the bank to view the scenery from a respectable distance?

That nasty little voice of intuition. She pointed out that I was wrong in how I was engaging in communication with Frogs who were actually interested in me. To them, I could have been The One. To me, they were ways to end lonely nights at home, helping me pass the long hours. My intuition was absolutely right and at that moment, I hated her. Which is why I made the choice to continue with Rick even though it made absolutely no sense. She, my noise-making voice of intuition, wanted me to stop playing it safe. She wanted me to get out of that chair and go meet some Frogs in person. So that is exactly what I would do. Who knew that the same voice of intuition would be back in a month to tell me in her grating, high pitched voice, "You are a lunatic! What in the world are you thinking?!"

Rick was a fun and engaging guy, and we hit it off immediately. He lived outside the city in a log cabin he was remodeling on a few acres of land. Although his home life was kind of rustic, he worked for a telecommunications company in a nearby town, but preferred the quiet country life. I could relate to this as I was raised on a cattle ranch and grew up with the whole package: horses, cows, pigs, chickens, turkeys. Planting a garden, cutting our own wood, baling hay, harvesting our garden and moving sprinkler pipe by hand in the summer. Yes, a true country girl living in the city, but those roots run deep. Rick, on the other hand, was raised in the city but wanted to escape the madness, so he'd decided to live in the country and commute. I could see the appeal. And he was likewise impressed that I could relate to everything he was trying to achieve or was enjoying in his rural home life.

After a few weeks of emails, which graduated to long phone conversations at bedtime, Rick and I found we had a real connection. He was divorced without children and, well, you know my story. He had served in the Marines, so we had that military bond in common – although he gave me a lot of grief about being in the wimpiest branch of the service one could ever choose to be in. This was not a new topic for me as my little brother is a former Marine and I'd already heard every joke and comment there was comparing the Air Force to the Marines. Funny how neither one of them stuck it out to retirement, but I was able to. Guess it's because of how soft the pillows are in the Air Force and the superior food served in our dining halls. Yup, we want to join the Marines but we don't want to necessarily stay. Hoorah!

So, Rick and I decided to finally meet. Our communication had grown to talking to each other on the way to work every morning as well as at bedtime. We invested about an hour of conversation per day together and it really felt like we had learned a lot about each other over the course of four to five weeks. It was certainly time to take things up another level and look into his eyes while I let him gaze with wonder into mine. We made plans for our first date in two weeks over a long holiday weekend. We were finally going to meet in person and see if sparks would fly and stars collide. It was time. And I don't mind saying I was giddy with excitement.

So I bought my round trip plane ticket to North Dakota. North Dakota!? What the hell? Did I just say I was buying a ticket to North Dakota? I may have been raised in Montana, but I now lived in Texas. That is a very long journey for a mere three-day weekend. I know what you're thinking, too. I have just bought a ticket to fly to North Dakota to spend a long weekend with a man that I don't actually know. I've spoken to him for hours on end, seen pictures of him and gotten countless emails from him. But fly to North Dakota to meet Rick and spend the long weekend in his cabin in the woods? Alone? Didn't this take things just a step beyond going over to Sal's house? At least there I had been able to walk out the front door and go right home.

Yes, my little bitch of reason was having an absolute, full blown, and bigger than life hissy fit at that very moment. Screaming inside my head with her grating voice. Of course, it didn't happen when I was talking to Rick on the phone in the mornings on the way to work or at night snuggled in my bed. No, she was silent at those times. But the other 14-15 hours of my day, there she was. Taunting, pleading and threatening. "You are crazy, Rose!" she screamed. "You don't know this guy. What if he never lets you come home again? What if he doesn't look like his picture? Didn't you learn anything from the Sal experience? He could drug you, torture you and bury you behind the woodpile. Have you lost your ever loving mind?" There was no shutting this voice up.

And then I started thinking about the situation rationally instead of emotionally. Did I really know Rick? No. Was there even the slightest possibility that anything he said could be false? Yes. Was there the remotest chance that I could be putting myself in danger by traveling alone to this man's home to spend the weekend with him? Absolutely. Was I taking things just a little too far after being called a fraud and a fake for my involvement in internet dating at that time? Yes indeed. My voice of reason and intuition was absolutely right – and I had three days left before boarding that plane to go meet Rick in North Dakota. It was time to end the screaming, hysterical voice of lunacy in my head before I killed her.

The next morning as I drove to work, my phone rang at 7 a.m. as was typical for my new routine with Rick.

"Good morning beautiful," he said. "I'm so excited for your trip! I've been cleaning out the guest room for you."

My heart sank, as I knew it was time to ask the one question that would end this madness and shut up the crazy lady in my head.

"Rick, if we hit it off and find we are compatible," I said, "are you willing to move to Texas?" I felt nerves shooting electricity through my car interior.

There was silence on the other end as my voice of reason (and sanity) and I held our breath. And thankfully, there were no screaming voices inside my head for the very first time in weeks.

"Would you move to Texas to be with me?" I asked again.

Still no sound.

I continued, "I ask because I won't leave Texas. My son, my sisters, my niece and nephew, and my friends are all here. I have a great job and love this area. I could not move to North Dakota. Ever." I heard the crazy lady actually sigh with relief.

Finally, Rick broke the silence and admitted that he wouldn't leave North Dakota, either. He was happy there and simply couldn't relocate to be with me.

Of course, this wasn't a surprise to me. It wasn't that I had refused to listen to him as we had spent hour after hour sharing our lives on the phone. I knew completely that he was at home in North Dakota. He knew that I was equally at home in Texas. We simply ignored those voices inside our heads and moved forward with emotions only. This is not only foolish, but dangerous.

I had heard the warnings that my intuition screamed out loudly about risk taking and danger, and being buried behind the woodpile. The voice in my head is one loud nasty bitch when she wants to be. She knocked me around from the start for misrepresenting my reasons for being on the dating websites, and then she kicked me back to reality when I thought there was a Frog in North Dakota that had Prince Charming printed on his birth certificate. The funny thing is that I had known better and proceeded anyway. Ultimately, I lost a fairly significant amount of money by canceling that plane trip; however, I finally came to my senses and realized that my decision making at that time was not rational or well thought out. Unfortunately, it wasn't my only experience with knowing better from the start and continuing anyway with false expectations.

Let me share with you a different experience about intuition and that crazy lady in my head. However, with this tale we will add a dose of lowering personal standards as well. When one ignores the voices that give guidance and reason but adds the unfavorable trait of minimizing expectations, it's simply not going to end well. With that in mind, into my life entered Chip.

My first communication with Chip was different than most I'd received, as he had already seen me out in public when he came across my dating profile. It just so happened that we were on leagues at the same bowling alley on the same weeknight; however, we were on different leagues that started within a half hour of the other. He was typically at the far end of the bowling alley while I was towards the opposite end. I had seen him several times and noticed the way he would glance over at me as he passed by on his way to the bar or restroom. He would smile, I would smile back, and some flirting passed through the air each time. I figured he was married or otherwise unavailable, and didn't give him much thought until he contacted me online.

When I received his first email, I knew exactly who he was. Chip playfully inquired as to why a girl like me needed to be on a singles website and said he thought it was a shame. I replied that if guys would "man up" and do something besides walk by and stare when they went to the bar or restroom, perhaps I wouldn't have to be. That was all it took.

The following Monday night during our league, Chip did something different as he walked towards the bar to get his team some drinks. He still smiled at me, but he did it while he approached our team's table at our lane. This handsome, mysterious man was headed directly towards me like a man with a mission! We had never spoken to each other except to say hello in passing, so this was one of those moments when the butterflies began to spread their wings and bat furiously against my stomach lining. In fact, they seemed to be trying to escape through my throat and into my mouth!

"Hello Rose," Chip said as he extended his hand. "Would you like to get together this weekend to do something fun?"

'Oh, be still, my heart, and please don't let me stutter when I reply,' I told myself. 'Please also let my palm be dry, and not sweaty and sticky, as I shake his hand.' "Absolutely, yes, and thank you for asking," I replied without missing a beat.

We exchanged phone numbers, he promised to call later that week to make plans, and off he went to complete his secondary mission at the bar. My girlfriend and I giggled and acted like silly girls do when something unbelievably exciting happens, like a good looking guy seeking out a girl he is interested in and asking for a date. We also noticed that his buddies on his team clapped him on the back and smiled generously when he returned with their drinks and the news that he had secured a date with me.

Chip did as he promised by calling later that week to share his plans for our first date: Dinner at a very nice restaurant that overlooked the lake with many decks to enjoy the sunset, food and live music. I was excited for the week to end and, of course, it crawled along at a snail's pace.

Friday finally came, and the first date began. Everything went fabulously from the moment he showed up at my house to pick me up. He complimented my lovely home, he opened the car door for me, and he called me "sweetheart." Bonus – he smelled absolutely fantastic.

Great music played on his car stereo that we both sang out loud to with no reservations or embarrassment. We both displayed our best "upper body moves" by dancing in our seats and laughed. As we looked up through his sunroof at the beautiful evening sky, the moon was just peeking out for the evening. Chip had been in the Air Force during a portion of the same time that I was, and we had a great conversation about our experiences in the military on the way to the restaurant.

We arrived at the beautiful destination and walked hand in hand into the restaurant as the sun was setting. Dinner was delicious, the atmosphere was relaxing and romantic, and Chip was a perfect gentleman. We shared great conversation during dinner as we listened to the live music and enjoyed the atmosphere. Our conversation was engaging and fun on the way back to my house, and the evening seemed almost fairy tale perfect.

We ended the evening slow dancing in my driveway (under the stars, as my landscape lighting shined up into the tree canopy) to a wonderful slow song played on his car stereo. How romantic is that? Really, slow dancing in the dark on the driveway! It couldn't have been a more perfect first date. There were absolutely no screaming voices in my head, nor any warning signs that this man might not actually be my Prince Charming. I certainly enjoyed kissing this particular Frog that night while dancing closely together on my driveway. I was looking forward to getting to know him better to see where life would take us.

Unfortunately, the next date divulged information that changed the course of what was to be and caused me to lower my values and ignore my voice of reason.

When I saw Chip on Monday night at bowling, we acted like love struck teenagers. He texted me all night long from Lane 38, and I returned his texts from my vantage point on Lane 17. He complimented my legs, raved about our date Friday, and shared that his bowling buddies were quite jealous that he secured a date with me. I was equally flirtatious and enjoyed the attention and the moment. When our league ended, I walked down to where Chip's team was bowling to meet his buddies and tell him goodnight. We made plans for the following Saturday, as he had his daughters that next weekend and promised to call me later that week. 'How could this be more perfect?' I wondered.

We spoke during the week, he called on the weekend, and we repeated our flirting at bowling on Monday. I was excited, interested and looking forward to seeing Chip again.

Saturday came and it was time for our second date. I met Chip at his house, as he wanted to show me where he lived and give me a glimpse into his little corner of the world. He was divorced and had two adolescent daughters who he had custody of every other weekend. He was a devoted father and seemed to have a good relationship with his girls. He lived in a modest rental house on the other side of the town I lived in and introduced me to his two lovable dogs. I love dogs and had fun throwing the ball for them in the back yard. Chip offered me a beer and we played outside with the dogs, throwing the ball for a little longer while enjoying our drinks.

I had visions of togetherness, romance and a life spent with this wonderful, handsome Frog that I truly was interested in. Finally, the game of life was dealing me a great hand of cards and I looked forward to raking in the pot of gold in the center of the gaming table. Well, until my hopeful Prince Charming excused himself to go out into his garage and told me to make myself comfortable until he returned.

Well, this was quite awkward now, wasn't it? I stood in his kitchen looking around at his stove, refrigerator and dishwasher while he did God knows what in his garage. Changing the oil in his car, perhaps, or cleaning the windows before we left for our date to play pool with his friends? The minutes ticked by. I finished my beer and wondered what could be so important in the garage that he had to leave me standing in the kitchen.

Finally, Chip came back into the house. "Ready to go have some fun?" he asked.

Well, yes! I certainly was.

He finished his beer in one big swallow and off we went.

The evening was fun at the pool hall in a neighboring town. There was music playing, I met some of Chip's friends, and we enjoyed drinking a few beers and relaxing. Chip excused himself at one point and told me he'd be right back, walking out the door with a female friend.

Well, this was equally as awkward as standing in

Chip's kitchen as he did his secret task in his garage. Here I was with my beer in my hand surveying the patrons of this particular pool hall while my date was engaged in some sort of activity outside with a woman I didn't know, but who he seemed to know rather well. The fact that she was married and her husband was playing a game of pool right in front of me did nothing to dissuade the voices that started to chant inside my head. The husband certainly didn't seem concerned that my date and his wife had exited the establishment and left us to fend for ourselves in the pool hall. The loud voice had begun to speak her mind again and I was trying desperately not to listen. Clearly, there was more to Chip than I knew, and I wasn't certain I was going to be okay with whatever it was.

Within ten minutes, although it seemed like hours, Chip and his married female friend returned. I was not amused, and within the hour, we made our exit and headed towards his humble abode. The voices in my head were now ringing on high alert, at a volume loud enough to rupture eardrums. Why had he left me twice within a few hours, and what was this secret activity that he was so intent on completing? What was so secret about what he was doing that I couldn't be invited to join in either time he had left me alone? Something told me I was not going to like the answers if I asked the questions. But I was certainly going to ask them because I didn't like what my intuition was telling me.

"Would you like to stay for a little while?" Chip asked when we arrived back at his house.

"I'd be happy to," I said, since I did enjoy his company.

He walked me back into the kitchen and offered me a drink, which I accepted. As I stood in the kitchen yet again, Chip excused himself to go back out to the garage for a moment. What the hell? What could be so important in that garage where we had just parked that he had to leave me yet again?

Standing in the kitchen looking at the pictures and drawings on his refrigerator, I decided that I was not going to be excluded from whatever he was doing. Whether that was washing his windshield or putting out rat poison, I refused to stand in the kitchen as an outsider to his activities. The voice in my head was in full support of finding out exactly what was going on with this mystery man. 'Let's do something to end the mystery!' the voice said.

I nervously walked towards the garage door and pushed it open. "Hey, what's going on out here?" I asked.

As I entered the garage with my beer in my hand, it hit me. The unmistakable odor of pot permeating the closed interior of the garage. There stood Chip, leaning against his work bench with a pipe in his hand. He took another hit, tapped out the contents into a coffee can, and placed it in a drawer on the top shelf of his work bench as he blew out the smoke from his last drag. I was in shock. Chip, my future Prince Charming and special man of the moment, was a recreational drug user. At least at that moment I thought it was recreational, but was it?

We came back into the house and stood facing each other in the kitchen.

"Do you have a problem with the fact that I smoke pot?" Chip asked.

I was still reeling from the realization that this was part of his lifestyle and was trying to process the fact that it went against my grain. It dawned on me that Chip smoked pot before we went on our date to play pool, he likely left with his married female friend to do the same outside while we were out on our date, and then did the same thing immediately upon returning to his house. That equated to three pot smoking events in about a three hour period. This didn't speak to me as being recreational. At least, that's what that loud, obnoxious voice inside my head was screaming to me. And at that moment, I tended to agree with her.

As we looked each other over inside his house, I decided to ask the unpopular and direct question of Chip at that moment.

"How often do you do this?" I asked.

His response was not what I expected. "I do it for relaxation," he said. "I'm not addicted and I can give it up any time I want to."

My intuition voiced its distrust and skepticism in a screeching voice in my head. I couldn't help to agree with her, but oh … I really, really, really liked this particular Frog. Perhaps I was overreacting and it wasn't as it initially seemed? I let the subject go for the time and we tried to enjoy the rest of the evening together. He seemed to be in a state of relaxed euphoria, while I was anxious and uncertain. I didn't like the way his breath smelled after smoking pot. I had wanted to kiss this Frog, but not so much at that moment in time.

The evening ended and we said our goodnights. I was torn as the weekend continued and I replayed the date in my mind. How did I feel about dating someone who participated in this illegal activity (I know, there are many sides to this debate) since it had been engrained in me as off-limits due to my involvement in the military? Was it truly recreational or was it an addiction and, therefore, a problem? This had painted an entirely different picture on the canvas of my future Prince Charming.

I told my girlfriend about the dilemma and she agreed that it could be a problem. Here was a guy who, as a father, clearly had to pay child support and was renting a very small two bedroom, one bathroom home. He was partaking in an activity that is not entirely inexpensive depending on how often he participated. From my vantage point over the weekend, it certainly had seemed that Chip was a very active player in that game. I just wasn't sure if I was okay with it or not.

At bowling the following Monday, I tried to focus on the positives about Chip. I was very attracted to him, he was extremely sweet and complimentary, and we had a spark that was undeniable. The flirting by text continued through our bowling evening, and he stopped by our lane on his way to the bar to give me a hug and say hello to my girlfriends. I thought even more that he was very sexy and handsome. Perhaps I was overreacting regarding his recreational activity? No, not according to that voice still loudly objecting inside my head. Remember, I was retired from the military. This type of activity goes completely against my grain and ethical behavior. For twenty years I was subject to a random, no-notice drug test and had to provide a urine sample with an escort standing in the bathroom watching me on five different occasions. I saw peers of mine lose all their benefits and get dishonorably discharged from the military for a weekend tryst that was caught in a random drug test. I was so serious about staying clean that I wouldn't even associate with people who gambled with throwing the drug test dice by occasionally partaking in that activity. What was I going to do about this then?

Our next weekend together helped me make up my mind. Chip invited me over to his house to meet his girls and to barbeque hamburgers on the grill. I went with an open mind, a hopeful heart and with that annoying voice still reverberating inside my head. When Chip answered the door, both of his dogs and girls joined him to welcome me. It was a whirlwind of activity with barking and introductions and excitement as we all entered the house. The kitchen was full of preparations for dinner and I joined in to help with preparing the food. Chip's daughters were excited to show off for me as little girls always do when someone new is around. They were jumping around, squealing and vying for as much attention as I was able to give them as I cut tomatoes and onions while Chip started the grill.

"Would you like a beer?" Chip asked when he came in from the backyard.

"Sure, thanks," I said.

He pulled two beers out of the refrigerator, and we clinked bottles and said, "Cheers." Then Chip leaned over, kissed my cheek and said, "I'm going out into the garage for a moment, sweetheart. Would you entertain the girls in the house until I return?"

I could feel my heart fall through my stomach, down through my colon and end on my feet. His two little girls were there in the house, I was his guest visiting, and he was excusing himself to go out into the garage. I didn't even have to guess what for.

While Chip was in the garage, I chatted with the girls on the couch and they did their best to impress me with their shenanigans. Physically I may have been sitting on that piece of furniture listening to his girls; however, my heart was turning cold and in my mind, loud screaming voices would not be silent. This certainly wasn't cool and it absolutely wasn't recreational. I simply wasn't going to be able to overlook or accept this activity of his, but I also came to the realization that I was going to have to tell him. Considering the fact that I saw him every Monday night, I would have to come clean and be honest as to why I couldn't continue. I was not looking forward to it, but I certainly wanted the voices inside my head to shut the hell up.

After dinner was over, the kitchen was cleaned up and the girls were bathed for bed, we all cuddled on the couch to watch a movie. Naturally, I was a little more reserved than I may normally have been as I contemplated when to have the discussion with Chip about my inability to accept his activity in the garage. The girls fell asleep during the movie as energetic little girls often do, and Chip got them settled in their room while I stayed on the couch thinking. When he returned to the living room, he excused himself. Yes, to go out into the garage. That final act made my mind up with no hesitation.

When Chip returned to the living room and sat next to

me, again it was very obvious what he had been doing in the garage. It was time to come clean and voice my disapproval.

"How often do you smoke pot?" I asked.

"I do it to relax," he said immediately.

That didn't answer my question so I kept pushing. "I'm uncomfortable with it, and I'm shocked that you would do it when your girls are around."

"Ah, I can give it up anytime," Chip said. "It just helps relax me and relieve stress."

"Do you do it before you go to work? Give me a rundown of a typical day," I said. "Say, Monday."

"I don't smoke before work, but sometimes I do at lunchtime," he said. "Me and one of my bowling teammates smoke a little in the car before bowling, and then I usually do it when I get home afterwards." (Keep in mind that he also drank the entire time he bowled.)

This was a Frog that I wasn't sure I'd ever been around when he wasn't impaired in one way or another. I had a problem with that, as I typically lived each day sober. Unless I was going out with the girls, and then we drank responsibly. Now, mind you, I am not a teetotaler nor do I stand in judgment over what others do in their own lives – as long as it doesn't impact mine. What I am, however, is extremely selective about the types of individuals I let into my life and personal space. This is a very important part of personal choice and values. That is exactly why my raging lunatic intuition was having such a fit about my relationship with this particular Frog. His activities in the garage went completely opposite of what I could and would allow into my world. It made no sense to delay the inevitable.

Chip wasn't pleased with my decision to stop seeing him. He didn't argue with me or give any excuses for his activity. He knew my mind was made up. It did make it a little tense at bowling, but he was still friendly and sweet to me. It was difficult because every time I looked at him, my heart hurt. I was very much interested in him, but it just wouldn't have worked between us. One of his bowling teammates cornered me a few months after we stopped dating and asked me what happened. I answered that I was certain Chip had given him enough information to understand why. He claimed that Chip wouldn't tell them anything only that I had decided to stop seeing him. I simply said that our lives didn't mesh. Our personal choices were on two different pages, but I truly liked him and was sad that chapter ended. There was no need to drag him through the mud. It just was what it was.

The next bowling season, Chip didn't return to his league except as a substitute. I didn't get to see him very often over the next few years, and I missed his cute smile and his endearing ways. However, the voice in my head quieted immediately after my conversation with Chip, and I know that I did the right thing. I did the best thing for me in my life. I could have ignored the voices, continued to see Chip, and waited to see where it would take us. I would have lowered my standards, disregarded my personal values and put a muzzle on the raving lunatic in my head. But both you and I know that it would have eventually ended in a very ugly way. That's simply not the way I wanted that chapter in my life (or his) to end.

We hear voices, get feelings and have a certain set of

personal standards for a very good reason. These are our guiding principles and even guardian angels, if you so believe. Every single time I've listened to my intuition – yes, that voice in my head or those times the hairs on my neck stand straight up – I am thankful for doing so. She has never let me down. Additionally, she has never been wrong. I, on the other hand, have definitely been wrong when I ignored her.

Listen to yourself and take those voices seriously. If you meet a Frog and you have to force the relationship to make it work, let him go. If that inner voice is screaming that there is something wrong with a certain Frog (meaning he may very well end up being a Toad), throw him back. Keep looking. If you have to lower your principles or values in order to be with a particular Frog, please don't. And by all means, do not pursue a dead end. You deserve to find someone who compliments your life, adds value to the very special Princess (or Prince) that you are, and can do it all without compromising your core principles. When the voices in your head begin to make noise, please listen with both ears wide open. 🐸

SOME FROGS ARE ACTUALLY TOADS. ACCEPT THAT AND MOVE ON

When a girl is kissing Frogs trying desperately to find her Prince Charming, she doesn't initially pay much attention to whether this particular Frog or that particular Frog could actually be a Toad. In the beginning, the differences can be quite easy to overlook. Very subtle differences indeed. There are so many things about Frogs and Toads that are very similar; it's quite easy to confuse the two. It's not until you get up real close and personal, spend some time with them and pay attention to the very little details that one actually notices the true differences. They both have the same amount of appendages, have two eyes, a mouth, tongue and share similar movements; however, the Toad can be more aggressive and quite ugly after the first glance. Toads are not a pleasant experience.

I met such a Frog – correction, I met such a Toad – while searching for my Prince Charming, who impacted me in many ways. While I didn't meet him online, my experience meeting him is significant enough to share with you. Some experiences with this person were actually very good, but there were the not so good experiences as well. For a period of time, I actually thought he might be The One. Yes, I actually believed he might be my Prince Charming and would put an end to this nonsense of having to kiss Frogs. However, there was eventually some downright ugliness about the interaction with this particular Toad that became quite unacceptable. I'll let you be the judge of whether you agree about my classification of Farad as this story unfolds.

Farad, an unusual name, yes ... and an equally unusual and very intriguing man as well. My first encounter with Farad was at a local nightclub during the very early beginnings of my newfound singleness. We danced together several times. We both happened to be out with friends and there was an instant attraction from across the room. Finally, after a few times of seeing each other periodically out dancing, he asked for my number after we had danced together. We didn't speak very much at the club – much too loud, and we were there to dance, right? But Farad said he'd call me on the following Tuesday to make plans for a date. He was different, foreign and very handsome. I was interested. Very interested indeed.

I remember the night he called quite vividly. I was standing in my kitchen leaning over the sink while looking out at the front yard. Listening to Farad on the phone, I realized he had very broken English and seemed to stumble over his words. The conversation was difficult and awkward, but we were able to communicate well enough to make plans for dinner on Saturday evening. He wanted me to meet him at his brother's Italian restaurant downtown. He said he'd call me again on Friday evening to decide what time to meet, and there we were. We had a date for dinner. I was now very interested, although I wasn't thrilled about driving downtown alone. But I could put aside those fears to meet this particular Frog in a quiet, romantic atmosphere. It was time to put the big girl panties on and do something different.

Friday came, but no call. I was not amused. I had

stayed home that night specifically to take his call. Saturday came, no date. I was disappointed. I was very certain what we were supposed to do, so clearly it was something on his side that caused the date not to happen. I didn't have his number, so there was no way to contact him. I wondered why he had decided not to call me when he very certainly seemed interested.

Weeks disappeared behind me, then months passed, even years went by and I continued to kiss Frogs looking for my Prince. I didn't see Farad again until several years later. Once again, we were out dancing on a Saturday night at a new dance place. I was having a blast with my girlfriends out on the dance floor, laughing, dancing. We were just single girls out having fun. And then, after all these years, there he was. Standing alone on the side of the dance floor, wearing jeans, a starched white shirt and looking out at me across the multitude of dancing bodies. Smiling. Looking just as handsome as he had so many years earlier. Maybe even more so. I froze, or at least my heart did.

What's a girl supposed to do in a situation like this? First thing: whatever you do, keep dancing! Don't let him think his presence has you flustered. It didn't matter that I had been interested in him so many years ago. It didn't matter that I was still very attracted to him. It certainly made sense that I was a little discombobulated, but what was I supposed to do? Then it came to me. There was only one thing I could do. I turned my back to him. Just kept dancing and ignored the fact that he was standing over across the room looking at me like a wolf eyeing the chicken coop. Did he really know who I was? Did he remember me from that many years ago? He must have remembered me! Why else was he standing there smiling and staring? The song ended, another one started, and we girls kept dancing. I kept my back to Farad, the handsome guy who got away.

But oh, dear Lord, help me. There he was. Standing right in front of me on the dance floor, smiling and looking way too hot for words, while my girlfriends and I continued to dance. He smiled like I should have been happy to see him. What? He wanted to dance with me now? Some nerve this man had, right? Wait, there went my girlfriends, walking off the dance floor waving and smiling. I stood there all alone with the guy who fully expected me to dance with him. He had balls, I'd give him that! I thought of just walking off the dance floor, showing him my best "you can kiss my butt" exit, and never speaking to him again! Is that what I did, you ask? No. So there I was, dancing with Farad. I was mad, I was not smiling at him, but oh, he was still smiling at me. And he smelled so very good. The song continued and, yes, I was still dancing with him. And, unfortunately I was actually enjoying it.

The night went on and we kept dancing together to every single song. Eventually my girlfriends decided to leave. They waved from the side of the dance floor, and I waved back and gave them the thumbs up sign that all was well. Farad and I continued dancing, but all the while he knew I was mad at him as I wouldn't warm up to his charms and refused to smile at him. We stopped dancing to get a drink.

"I will never forgive you for standing me up so many years ago," I finally said.

"I understand," Farad said. "I'm sorry. Back then, I only knew a few sentences in English, just enough to get a girl to dance with me and give me her phone number. I was afraid to meet you for dinner because we wouldn't have been able to talk. What would we talk about when I didn't know English? I really liked you and didn't want to ruin it."

Really? That wasn't ruining it? The jury was still out on that one.

So he had stood me up and then avoided me for the next several years while he built a business and learned English. Now there he was and, darn it, I was still interested. Remember the old saying, "If I knew then what I know now?" Yes, if I had known that night what the future would bring by getting to know Farad better, I'd have ended it after the last song played on the dance floor that night. I'd have stood him up on our next planned date and called it even. I would have never, ever kissed that Toad. Ever! Dang it all anyway.

Like a gentleman should when her girlfriends all leave before she does, Farad walked me out to my car when the dancing ended and the club closed.

"I want to see you again soon," he said. "I'll meet you anywhere."

"You'll just stand me up again," I said, pouting. "You won't show up. You'll break my heart again, and then I'll hunt you down like an animal and kill you."

"No, I promise this time will be different," he said.

I caved in and agreed to a date. Secretly, I was thrilled but still apprehensive.

Our first date was agreed upon for the following day –

Sunday evening. I figured I'd see if he was really interested in me. Would he go with me to a baseball game and sit next to me for nine innings? I would hold him hostage and even make him ride with me there. He said he didn't care what we did, he just wanted the chance to get to know me. So it was set. We met the next evening in a convenient parking lot near McDonald's at 6:15 p.m. He pulled up in his flashy Mercedes C Class, parked and then jumped in my car with me. He looked good and smelled even better. There is simply nothing like a handsome man who smells good. And off we went to enjoy a nice summer evening watching baseball.

This part of the story goes very well. We had a wonderful time at the baseball game but I don't think we saw any part of it or even knew who won. Engrossed in conversation and drinking cold beer, we shared many stories about our upbringing, personal history and life experiences with each other. Farad was attentive, sweet and very intriguing. This was a man who was not just sharing about his life but was interested in mine. He asked a lot of questions, seemed sincerely engrossed in what I had to say, and shared personal details about himself. He had been a member of the Iranian military and fought in the Iraqi war. He showed me two large, ugly scars where he was shot by a sniper in the left calf – a shot that could have been to his head if the sniper had wanted to kill him. It was his lucky day, he said. More stories continued about his older brother who had been in the United States for many years and encouraged him to come to America. He was very close to becoming a citizen and was proud to have been able to invest and open up a small local business. He lived very close to me in a neighboring subdivision and it all looked very promising. I was increasingly more interested as the evening passed and was happy I had given him another chance. Who knew where this would eventually lead!

We went on several more dates (mostly dinner dates), and spent a lot of time talking and getting to know one another. We only saw each other on the weekends due to his work schedule, but that was fine for me. I kept busy with work, walking mile after mile with my girlfriend, going to baseball games in the evening and occasionally going out with the girls. We did spend time in the evenings on the phone catching up with each other and getting to know one another.

He told me we weren't "dating" and that I shouldn't call him my boyfriend. No commitment, he said. Okay, I could live with that. Then a week later he said I was his girlfriend. Oh! Okay, now I was his girlfriend. But we couldn't say those three little words to each other, as he wasn't ready for a commitment. He had been single way too long and he liked it that way. But he did want to continue seeing me. I could live with that, too. Then, during a phone conversation a week later, he told me he loved me. Wait ... what? No. He. Didn't! Yes, he sure did. I didn't return the verbal sentiment as I was a little slower to let my guard down and fall for that little number, but I did acknowledge that I heard him by saying "Oh you do, do you?" I was still very interested and this guy had potential. 'Could he be my Prince Charming?' I wondered. He certainly did seem to have fallen for me quickly!

Now, during this timeframe, my girlfriend told me

she didn't trust Farad. "Something isn't right about him," she said, "I just know it won't end well." Her intuition, that voice in her head that screamed he was a Toad, was spot on. It took me a little longer to fully realize this fact. But I continued to see Farad and I enjoyed spending time with him. Handsome, attentive and interesting – I liked being with him. I was open for whatever the future would bring.

We had plans to go out one particular Saturday evening when Farad asked me to spend the night at his house. A sleepover! Our first one. This was quite a milestone for him, as he simply didn't do sleepovers. Why?

"Purely selfish reasons," he explained. "For one, I've always been a playboy and haven't found anyone special to spend time with. My only day off is Sunday, and it's my only day to sleep in and relax, so I never let any of my lady friends spend the night. Sunday is my day."

Any of his ladies who made it as far as returning to his house on a Saturday night found themselves escorted to the front door at a very early hour with the excuse that he had to work the next day. He admitted that he lied to them, but he did it so that he would not have to share his bed all night long, and so he could sleep in and not wake up the next morning to entertain someone. Selfish, yes. Lying, yes. Set in his ways, again, yes. He was quite open about his past activities and bad treatment of the ladies. I was actually impressed that he would be so upfront about his brazen behavior of women. His attitude was that he came first and everything else came second. Nothing hidden in that agenda, right? Right. But there we were, taking part in another milestone and going down a path that he typically didn't travel down. I was spending the night! I was special!

Excited, I packed my overnight bag, made sure all was well at my house a few miles away, and off I went to Farad's house for our very first sleepover. One benefit to this little idea was that I could enjoy myself, drink a little more wine than usual and relax with this handsome fellow who continued to keep me interested. The evening went perfectly. Farad even made room in his two car garage so I could park my little convertible that I loved inside. He cooked a nice dinner for us, and we spent time talking and cuddling on the couch, drinking wine and listening to wonderful music. It was romantic. It was sweet. It was easy.

Naturally, a very first sleepover brings some anticipation of breaking one's routine and trying to fit unobtrusively into someone else's habits and life. Which side of the bed did he usually sleep on? Should I take all my makeup off and let him see my true self, the un-enhanced version? If I didn't, would I get mascara and makeup all over his pillowcases? Would I be able to go to sleep at all? Would my little dog be fine without her momma at the house all night? Little did I know, these questions were not at all what I should have been worrying about as we prepared to end our first evening and go to bed.

Surprisingly, I was able to fall asleep quite quickly and easily, which is unusual given that it was my first night in a strange house. I didn't wake up during the night, I didn't toss and turn. I slept soundly the whole night through and when I woke up the next morning, it was to find that I was all alone in Farad's bed. I sat up and looked around the bedroom. Where was Farad? Perhaps he was in the bathroom taking a shower? 'He obviously doesn't sleep in as he claims he likes to do on Sunday mornings,' I thought. 'It's only 7:30 in the morning and he is up already!?' Oh, maybe he had just gotten up to use the bathroom and would return to the bed and back to me shortly. I lied there, looking around the room as signs of the morning sun made an appearance, listening intently to see if I could hear him in the bathroom. Shower running? Nope. Toilet flushing, perhaps? Nope again. Extreme silence. Not a sound in the house. It was odd. Where could he have gone?

I glanced over towards the bedside table next to me and saw my phone. Its green indicator light was flashing, telling me I had received a text or voice message since going to bed. Naturally, being the respectful person that I was and not wanting to disturb Farad during the night, I had put it on silent before going to sleep the night before. I wondered who it could be. Hopefully nothing had happened with any of my family. I checked the phone. What? It was a voice message. I was glad I'd turned the sound off on my cell phone. I would not have wanted to wake him in the middle of the night. But a voice message from whom? I looked at the caller ID. What the ever-loving hell? Farad? A voice message from Farad? Why would he have called me and left me a voice message? I was right there in his house! We had said our goodnights at the early hour of 1 a.m. when we had retired for the night. I was extremely curious as I entered my access code; however, the blood drained from my bright, shiny morning face as I began to listen to his message.

"You have one new voice message, recorded this

morning at 2:37 a.m. Beeeep. – Honey, its Farad. I'm sleeping in the other bedroom. No one can sleep through this. Listen."

And then I was greeted by the absolute, unmistakable sound of my own snoring. I was listening to a recording of myself snoring on this early Sunday morning as I lied alone in that man's bed while he slept in his guest room. Not just five seconds of recorded snoring, either. The recording went on for thirty-seven seconds. More than half a minute of unattractive and obtrusive snoring left on my own cell phone by this man in the middle of the night. I was shocked. I was flabbergasted. I was embarrassed. I couldn't help it, I had to play the voice message again as if it would be different the second time. Unfortunately, it didn't change. Yes, I was still snoring and it still lasted thirty-seven long, agonizing seconds. I was completely humiliated.

I started to think about the true totality of what Farad had done, and I started getting mad. No, not just mad. PISSED. One of those pissed off feelings that make you want to choke the ever-loving life out of someone. Yes, I have been told that I snore – mainly when I lie on my back or have a little too much wine to drink. I was sure I'd done both of those last night while sleeping next to Farad. But, I must now ask you this: What would be considered proper etiquette at a time like this when someone new is lying next to him snoring in bed late at night? The same someone new that he had called his girlfriend. The exact same someone new that he'd said "I love you" to. Did he nudge her? Wake her up and ask her to roll over, pretty please? Maybe plug her nose for a few seconds to see if she'd stop or roll over.

If that didn't work, perhaps kick her once or twice. Hard. That's always worked for me. But to deliberately pick up his cell phone, call the other person's phone while she lied in bed next to him, wait for the greeting to end and at the sound of the beep, say, "Honey, its Farad. I'm sleeping in the other bedroom. No one can sleep through this. Listen." And to then deliberately hold that same phone down to the gaping, opened mouth of the person lying next to him in bed loudly snoring for THIRTY-SEVEN MOTHER F'ING seconds? Who in their right mind would do that, anyway?

I was paralyzed with anger. What I should have done was jump out of this bed and gone to find him, wherever he was hiding inside that now seemingly cold, unwelcoming house of his. I wanted to scream obscenities, throw heavy or sharp objects at him, and maybe even strangle him until his eyes bulged and he finally stopped breathing. A little extreme? Not from my current vantage point as I stared at my phone and remembered how awful it felt to hear myself snoring on my own voicemail. It was even more painful to realize that this man, the man I'd had such hopes for a future with, was cruel and selfish. Completely unacceptable. I was crushed.

This story doesn't end here. Sometimes the best part of a story begins as the worst of it peaks. That's how we move on, heal our heart and find the humor in an otherwise unforgiving situation. That morning ended, I left Farad's house with my tail tucked between my legs, tears running down my face and spurts of anger causing me to cuss like a foul mouthed man hater as I hit my fists on the steering wheel on the drive home. I called my girlfriend who had known he was not what I had hoped he was. She threatened to go beat the holy crap out of him. I cried, I mourned and I felt sorry for myself. I never wanted to see him again. I didn't want an apology. I refused to take his calls. And he did call. He apologized in endless voice messages he left for me. He said I could get help, see a doctor, there were cures for snoring, and it didn't have to end there. He loved me. He wanted me to accept his apology. I, on the other hand, wanted nothing to do with that man. He was dead to me.

Time passed and the phone calls and texts finally ended as Farad realized there was no hope of a future with me. I shared my story with my sisters and my girlfriends. Naturally, they were appalled. "We have to get back at him! He must pay for his cruelness!" they said. No one should be allowed to treat someone they claimed to care for with such unabashed disregard and lack of sensitivity. But there was really nothing we could do to hurt him. My girlfriend and I drove by Farad's house one Saturday night very early in the morning when he might have been entertaining a young lady who clearly wouldn't have been sleeping over. We honked loudly, revved the engine and yelled out the car windows, "Loser!" We laughed, we giggled and a tiny, little bit of my heart healed. It was a simple thing but it felt so good. It felt like revenge on a very small scale. What I was craving was revenge on a large scale, but short of stringing Farad up naked in the center of town and throwing rotten fruit at him or burying him in fire ants, that wasn't going to happen. However, an opportunity was about to present itself that would be an acceptable second to the revenge that I craved.

It happened on a Saturday night several months later. We girls were out dancing after having margaritas at our favorite Mexican restaurant. Great drinks, good friends and loud music. We were back dancing at the same dance club that Farad visited regularly on Saturday nights. There were five different clubs in one large building where each room played a different genre to satisfy the masses. This was the same club where I ran into him when the good part of this story began. Secretly, I knew eventually, sooner or later, our paths would cross again. The question was not actually if we would run into each other, but how we would react when we did. I still wanted to hurt him. Physically. Immensely. Cripplingly.

Dancing, laughing and enjoying that particular girls' night out, we were having a blast. It was all about the music, the laughter and being together. As we danced in the Old School Room, I took a quick journey to the bathroom alone. Leaving the floor with my girlfriends still dancing, I walked through the adjoining Techno Room. The Techno Room always had loud music, lots of people and an air of excitement. Before I left the women's restroom, I decided to primp. May as well take care of all your business while you're in there, right? I pulled out my bright red lipstick from my purse and leaned in close to the mirror. A girl's wardrobe is just not complete without the lips being perfect. Yes, by the way, I admit that this was the same restroom where, a few months before, I had used a Sharpie to write some not so very ladylike things about Farad on the bathroom stall's wall. Yes, it was premeditated. I typically didn't go out dancing with a Sharpie in my purse. That's what anger, humiliation and a few margaritas will do to a scorned woman. But that wasn't to be the only form of revenge that evening.

When I was finished, I headed back out to return to my girlfriends to continue dancing the night away. As I was strutting through the room, I glanced to the right. And there he was. Farad. Standing on the other side of the dance floor gazing out across the moving bodies. Dressed in his jeans, his starched white shirt and smelling simply wonderful, I was certain. It was at this point that I hauled ass in my hooker heels out of the Techno Room and back into the Old School Room before he saw me. A girl can really move in high heels when she wants to or if she needs to.

"He's here! He. Is. Here!" I screamed, rushing onto the dance floor where my friends were still enjoying moving to the dance music. "Farad is here!"

Naturally, the music was too loud for them to hear me, so the screaming continued with no one understanding what was going on. We exited the dance floor and gathered at our table. Once they were all informed that the disgusting perpetrator was in the building, we devised our evil plan of revenge. It was quite simple, actually. I'd hit him where it hurt the most. Although I'd had many fantasies of running outside to the parking lot and keying his silver Mercedes, I knew that wouldn't nearly have hurt him enough. And, unfortunately, it could have been any number of girls he may have pissed off. There is only one way to hurt a man like Farad where it truly counts. Luckily, we knew exactly where that one spot was. In the pocket book!

It was at that very moment that Farad entered the Old

School Room through another door and walked up to the bar to get himself a drink. He leaned against the counter looking handsome and collected. Farad surveyed the available female menu, just waiting for his tasting pleasure, and, unfortunately, his eyes stopped their grazing directly on our table. To be exact, his eyes stopped directly on me. I froze. And Farad smiled. The nerve! I refused to smile back. I turned my head and steeled my heart. It was time to put our delightful little plan into action. Time to return the pain and suffering – as much as was legal. One of my girlfriends, Tamar, left our table and headed directly towards Farad at the bar. She had taken the role of our enforcer. She would deliver the revenge on a dish best served cold.

Farad looked collected and very cool as he smiled handsomely when she approached the bar. "Hi, honey," he said so graciously. "Can I buy you a drink?" Oh, yes – he was very smooth.

"Hi, Farad. No thanks. Remember me, though? Rose's friend?" Tamar said as he continued blessing her with an award winning smile.

The rest of us girls sat anxiously at the table and watched the show begin to unfold from our ringside seats. His smile was stunning; he was attempting to be so charming.

"Oh yes, I do remember you. How is Rose? I really miss her," he told my girlfriend. They both turned and looked towards our table. No one moved a muscle. I don't believe I was even breathing at that moment.

My girlfriend continued. "Rose is fine, Farad. But what you did to her was absolutely wrong and I've thought long and hard about it. You hurt her very badly and you need to be taught a lesson on how to treat women."

Farad looked confused and his smile faded just a little bit. "What do you mean?" he asked. "I tried to say I was sorry to her. What else can I do? She wouldn't take my calls or answer my texts."

"And she doesn't intend to, either, Farad. You were very hurtful and we," Tamar said as she motioned back towards our table, "believe that we need to warn other women about you."

The smile on his face faded a little more.

"I know you own a hair salon in my neighborhood as my teenage daughter has been to it. I shop in the grocery store right across the street. But even more importantly, I am a very active and outspoken parent on the PTA board of the high school just around the corner."

Farad side-stepped to the right and took a quick swallow of his drink. He obviously didn't like where this was going, and Tamar now had his full attention as she kept sharing her plan.

My girlfriend smiled, leaned in towards Farad and said, "You hurt my friend Rose very badly and in order to repay the favor, here is what I plan to do. There is a PTA meeting at the high school on Tuesday night next week."

The smile was now barely visible on his handsome face.

"Like I said, I am very active on the PTA board; therefore, I plan to make an announcement to the entire committee that you are of very low character and even lower class. I will explain that you treat women in an unfavorable manner and that your business should be avoided by all women. I will make sure that all those in attendance tell all of their friends to stay away from your salon as well."

He was listening intently now, stammered, and began to look seriously uncomfortable.

"We will all pass the word verbally and post it on Facebook. It will negatively impact your business, Farad," Tamar happily continued. "We can't harm you physically but, believe me, this will indeed hurt you."

He ran his hand over his forehead, glanced towards our table, and mumbled a few words.

"Maybe you'll remember this the next time you decide to treat a woman without care and respect." Tamar continued, "Think first before you decide to hurt the next woman. There are always consequences for your actions."

He was clearly stunned. Off-balance. Distraught. At that point, Farad stuttered, begged and pleaded. He declared his undying love for me and groveled for forgiveness. How could we be so cruel as to impact his business? His livelihood? It simply wasn't fair. My girlfriend stood silent – but smiling. With that, Farad, weak and confused, left the Old School Room in a very big hurry. My girlfriend proudly walked back to our table smiling from ear to ear to share what had happened. We girls then returned to the dance floor, smiling, laughing and emotionally renewed.

Revenge is sweet. How do you hurt a guy who needs to be taught a lesson? Hit him where it hurts. Make him think twice before messing with that group of girls again. Farad, being a business owner, had worked very hard to create a successful hair salon in that same neighborhood where my hard-hitting, verbal enforcing girlfriend Tamar lived. There are ways to get the message across. And what a message it was. You threaten his livelihood. Hit his pocket book. Impact his bottom line. Create havoc in the business he's worked so long to make successful. Although the message he was given during that verbal boxing match had no plans of being fully carried out, he didn't know that, did he? The plan was delivered with precision and conviction. Farad would have been a fool to doubt its authenticity.

Farad, my one time hopeful Prince Charming, was in reality nothing more than a hair cutting, root dying, snore recording Jerk Wad. This Toad, oh yes, he got the message. Very clearly. The proof was received on my cell phone, a voice message left by a very distraught salon owner the following morning. Of course, it came only after he had slept the night in his bed alone and woken up refreshed … or had he? "You have one new voice message, left today at 10:33 a.m. Beeeep. – Rose! Honey! It's Farad. Please. Call off your girlfriend. She threatened me. She is going to hurt my business. How can you do this to me? She plans to tell the entire PTA to stay away from my salon. Most of my business comes from that neighborhood. Please! I beg of you. Please call her off! I'm sorry. Please. Call me."

Oh, the despair. The concern. So much emotion in his voice. It was truly delicious and felt so revitalizing, simply refreshing and absolutely perfect. I wasn't able to get the type of revenge I craved for the way Farad had hurt me, but I did find satisfaction in knowing that what we were able to do to him had made an impact. After that, I could put that chapter behind me and bring to an end the memory of that first hurtful voice message from Farad. It was replaced by a brand new voice message of a different flavor. Revenge tasted so sweet.

Now, I'm not suggesting that revenge should be taken against every Frog that does us wrong. There is simply no way to win with that logic. However, what I suggest is that you go into every situation with the knowledge that things may not always be as perfect as they may initially seem. Every Frog has a story, a checkered past and perhaps dark corners in their closets. Yes, some of these men we kiss will be Toads rather than Frogs. Accept that. They may start out seemingly perfect, made just for you and cause dreams to enter your mind and heart of what could possibly be. At the moment you recognize this person is actually a Toad, let him go. Drop the disgusting thing back into the pond. Move on. Turn away and cut your losses. You deserve so much better. You deserve the one and true Prince Charming who is out there waiting just for you. Yes, he is out there. Keep. Kissing. Frogs.

SOME FROGS JUST DON'T HEAR NO THE FIRST TIME

There are Frogs that a girl will meet in her life that she clearly isn't interested in, she'll tell him exactly that, but he'll just keep hopping back onto her lily pad. Dan was just that Frog. One of the greatest shortfalls of internet dating is not really knowing who the person on the other side of the screen truly is. The dating profile shows one story, but there could be (and often is) a whole new saga waiting to be told when you meet in person. I'm not talking about someone actually being married and presenting himself or herself as single online. This happens, yes. More than we know and more than anyone admits. In fact, as unpopular as it may be to say this – if someone is married and their spouse is often busy on the computer or out at odd times, gets texts on their phone that no one else can read, or has an ironclad password to their email account – well, I'm just saying. One never knows. But back to Dan.

I liked Dan's profile online as he seemed like a real macho guy. His photos were fun and easy to see. I had no fear that he wouldn't look like his photos. He was sitting on a Harley in one of them and had a close up shot showing a handsome face and nice eyes in the other. We spent a few weeks corresponding with each other and he finally said he didn't want to just get to know me online – let's meet for dinner, he suggested. I agreed and we made a date for the following Friday night at a … yes, wait for it … Mexican restaurant close by. I arrived a little earlier than Dan and waited inside the front doors for him to arrive. I could hear him coming before he actually pulled into the parking lot. He was riding his Harley and, yes, it sounded like one. We all know that sound. I peeked out the door and watched him climb off his ride, place his goggles over the handle bar and start towards the restaurant entrance. 'So far so good,' I thought. Tall, attractive and manly looking. I was actually thinking the date might turn out to be pretty enjoyable after all.

When you meet one guy after another and things just don't work out, a girl tends to become a bit jaded about the whole dating scene. I would occasionally take my dating profile offline for several months while I recuperated from the experience of meeting guys who weren't my type, weren't who I thought they would be, or even who they thought they were. An online dating break from one disappointment after another. During those times I would concentrate on just going out with the girls as I became a little cynical, and that's never good when communicating with a potential Prince Charming. They expect the person on the other end to be just as excited to meet someone new as they are. Which brings me back to Dan.

Dan was very excited to meet me and at that very moment, I was equally excited. He stepped inside the restaurant, recognized me immediately, complimented me on truly looking like my profile pictures ("Even better!" he said) and off we went – escorted by the hostess to a booth in the dining room active with patrons on a Friday night. We sat across from each other taking the other person in, and it was obvious that Dan was more nervous than I was. He seemed a bit fidgety. It was kind of amusing, in a way, that he was so nervous. Here was this big Harley dude, and I was making him all discombobulated.

We ordered margaritas and the conversation began. Dan was polite and asked me a few questions about being in the military. The margaritas arrived, we loosened up a bit and Dan asked me if I thought it was hot in the restaurant as he wiped his forehead with his napkin. I looked at his face and saw that he was indeed sweating.

"No," I said as I looked around to see if anyone else at the other tables appeared to be over heated.

"Must be me," Dan said as he mopped his forehead again.

The waitress returned and we ordered dinner.

Dan looked across the table at me and said, "You are too far away. Let me move over there by you." He picked up his margarita, got out of his side of the table and slid into the booth next to me.

Now, I'm not usually anxious about people in my personal space, but this seating arrangement meant I had to look to my left in order to see Dan while he spoke to me. And he was very close to me! I enjoyed it better when he had been across the table from me! Not to mention he was still occasionally mopping at his forehead and face with a napkin. That napkin, by the way, was starting to come apart from all that sweat-soaking-up action. What the hell? If Dan was going to have a sweat storm, I preferred that he do it on the other side of the table. I couldn't concentrate. What was he saying? He worked as a contractor for a big computer company in town but they treated him like dirt. I could actually see the sweat dripping down his face. What? He wanted to know if he could use my napkin. Oh boy. This wasn't going well.

The waitress brought out our food and I suggested to Dan that he move back over to the other side of the booth. It would be much easier to eat that way. Oh, and waitress … can you bring us some more napkins or a big bath towel, please? I was starting to be concerned about Dan and all his body fluids escaping through the pores on his face. Eat some salt, Dan the Harley Man! Re-hydrate for God's sake.

We started eating our dinner and it became that time. Yes, time for another margarita. This was simply not a one-drink date. Dan ordered another margarita as well. And more napkins. He'd mopped his face so many times that little pieces of white fluff were sticking to his facial hair and forehead. I had the urge to reach across the table to remove the largest of those pieces stuck just above his left eyebrow, but I was afraid that would signal some tenderness and he would move back over to my side of the booth. I didn't want him dripping on my side. I'd become a little territorial about my space all of a sudden. This was the no-drip zone on my side of the table. Keep your sweating, dripping mess on that side, please. Thank you, Dan.

Now if this had been the end to the worst of the evening with Dan, we could have had a laugh and gone on our own way. It wouldn't have eliminated him from a future date (as long as that date was in a well ventilated or windy spot). However, the deciding factor for my realization that all was not kosher in the world of Dan came after dinner had ended and we were finishing our second margarita. That's when

Harley riding Dan decided to come clean and share. This was the information he hadn't put on his online profile.

"I'm not in a good spot in life since my divorce finalized a few months earlier," said Dan as he took another drink of his margarita. He continued to explain that the ex-Mrs. Dan had gotten the house, which she now shared with their son and the new man in her life, plus his son. Dan, on the other hand, was working the crappy contract job at the computer company down the road, paying child support and living with his sister. The sister didn't have an extra bedroom because she had four kids; therefore, he was sleeping on the couch in the living room. He was barely making ends meet and life hadn't been the biggest ball of fun for Dan.

Whoa! The sweating Dan sitting across the table from me wiping his wet forehead once again was clearly in a different place than I was. I had absolutely no drama, was financially secure with a nice four-bedroom house that I'd bought, and I truly loved my job. This simply wasn't going to work. But then wasn't the time to tell Dan that. I didn't need him passing out on me from stress, disappointment and dehydration on the other side of the table. I'd almost be obligated to do mouth to mouth – if I could get a good seal on that wet face, that is.

What does a person say at a time like this? A person like me, that is. Sitting across the table from Dan listening to his sad story while I watched that piece of soggy napkin still stuck on his eyebrow. Did I tell him, "Yes, I'm sorry. That's a tough gig. Things will get better for you," all the while thinking that, once again, this would be the first date that was also the last date? I was feeling disappointed and realized that I would have to start all over again. What I was always clear about when kissing Frogs is that I needed to find someone in the same financial and overall similar life situation that I was currently in. My Prince Charming needed to be on my level as an equal. Dan clearly was not even close to my level, and this was just not going to work. However, I needed to let him down gently and with kindness.

We finished our dinner, he paid the check and we walked out into the parking lot. Dan showed me his Harley, which he was very proud of, and then walked me over to my car. I was hoping for a nice handshake or a friendly hug to end the date. Dan had other plans, though. As we got to my car, he turned to me and asked the question I was hoping I wouldn't hear that night: "May I kiss you?" Let's see, was he still pouring sweat out of every facial pore he had? A quick look up confirmed that the coast was clear and his water works had finally ceased. That little piece of napkin had even disappeared from his eyebrow. Reluctantly, I told him yes and Dan bent down for a quick kiss. Nothing too intimate or serious. A nice soft pucker, and he kept his tongue safely inside his own mouth. A good way to end the night, I supposed. He opened my car door, bid me a good night and off I went – calling my girlfriend before I could even get out of the parking lot to tell her about the date and the sweat fest. We had a good laugh and she said, "Well, at least you won't have to see him again." Oh, little did we know how wrong that statement would be. And she would be right there alongside me to experience the horror of that next encounter.

Dan contacted me by email later that weekend and I broke the news to him. "I don't believe we are a match, based on the different points we are at in life at this time," I wrote. I wished him well and thanked him for a nice evening. I did not mention the sweat fest or specifics of his situation. Dan wrote back and said he didn't agree, wanted to see me again and begged for another chance. I tried to let him down gently and kindly. If only he would have left it at that, things would not have gotten ugly several months later.

Fast forward a few months when my girlfriend and I were sitting at a weekend baseball game, enjoying a warm summer night and a cold beer. I had season tickets for the AAA team in my town and spent a lot of time enjoying the baseball atmosphere, the comradery of the fans and spending time with my girlfriends. After many years of sitting in the same seats, I got to know many of the other season ticket holders around me and it was always like being with good friends. It was easy to pick out someone who was new to our section, which is why it took me only a minute that evening to spot Dan sitting at the end of my row. Oh, lucky me.

"That's him! Down at the end of our row!!" I whispered to my girlfriend.

"Who?" she asked, as she frantically looked around.

"Dan! Dan the Harley Man!" I told her anxiously.

"Oh yuck!" she said with disgust. "He's chewing and spitting it on the floor."

I took a quick glance down towards Dan and, sure enough, he was definitely chewing tobacco and he was most assuredly spitting on the floor in front of him. The same floor that we other fans would have to walk on to exit our row. 'Oh no he didn't,' I thought. Not on my watch. I would put a stop to that right then and there.

I marched my happy ass right up the aisle (going out on the other side, mind you) to the top of the section to let one of the ushers know what was happening in Section 114, Row 3. They proceeded to come down to inform the offender, AKA Dan the Harley Man, that he must use a proper receptacle if he planned to continue chewing, and he had to clean up the floor in front of him. I don't believe Dan knew it was me that turned him in, as he hadn't yet seen me. It wasn't long after that Dan picked up his spit cup, his beer and left our area. But that wasn't the last we would see of the former sweating and current tobacco-chewing Dan.

It seems Dan decided he needed to attend several games a week and always sat at the very end of our row. He finally recognized me during his next visit and said hello to me as I walked past him to go to the restroom. Later during the game, Dan came down the aisle behind me and sat down to talk with me for a bit. The good news was that he wasn't sweating or chewing, but the bad news was that he wanted to know in more detail why I wouldn't go out with him again. My girlfriend sat a few seats away from me rolling her eyes, listening to everything Dan had to say.

"You don't really want to hear this, Dan," I said. I really didn't want to say it. But Dan persisted and said he had a right to know. Finally, I gave in. I confessed. I shared with him exactly why I wasn't interested in pursuing another date.

"You're being superficial," he said. "I have a lot of potential! You know, I'm more than where I am in life right now."

"That's probably true, Dan," I told him, "but at this point in time, I'm not interested." What I didn't share with Dan was that now that I knew he chewed tobacco, it really sealed his fate as a non-option. Although he was a little miffed at the whole situation, he vowed he would not give up and that I would someday see what I was missing. Unfortunately, that day didn't take too long to come.

Fast forward to a few weeks later, towards the end of summer. It was another great Saturday night spent with that same girlfriend at the baseball field enjoying the game. We hadn't seen Dan over the past few weeks and I truly thought he was history. Not so much. The game had just started, the section was full of many people I knew, and the spirit was high for a weekend victory from our team. Out across the sea of noises from the game, a voice rang out. Not just a voice, much more than that. There he was – Dan, standing up at the end of the aisle yelling to me across the heads of my neighbors. It appeared Dan had had a few drinks of choice, as he was a bit unsteady on his feet and he was sloshing what certainly wasn't his first beer all over the seat in front of him. To make matters worse, as he yelled across the section to catch my attention, he did so with a huge, protruding wad of tobacco in the corner of his bottom lip.

"Rose! Hey, Rose!" he yelled, but with his slurred words and tobacco fattened lip, it sounded more like, "Woeth! Hey, Woeth!" He continued very loudly for all those sitting in our section to hear. "Rose! Do you like Barry?" with "Barry" sounding oddly like "Bawwy."

I tried to ignore him. People in front of me turned around to stare in my direction and look over to the yelling, beer-sloshing and tobacco-chewing Dan.

"Rose! I saaiid … Do you like Barry?" he yelled as he loudly emphasized each word. It was a small wonder that he didn't spit tobacco on the people around him as his lower lip was pushed out as far as it could go.

Oh Lord. If I didn't address Dan, someone was going to smack him. Why was he asking me about Barry? Barry who? Barry Bonds? I mean, we were sitting at a baseball game, so that made perfect sense to me. But why did he care if I liked Barry? "Barry who, Dan?" I called back, clearly disgusted, across the heads of my neighbors who were all listening intently. The game had now become secondary to the fans in Section 114. Dan and his antics had now taken the center stage and he had everyone's full attention. He was now definitely going to tell me who Barry was, I felt quite certain of this. I felt my muscles tensing up.

"Barry! The only Barry that ever did or ever will matter! Barry Manilow, that's the Barry!" he hollered back to me across the row.

Oh dear God. Help me, Jesus. Barry Manilow. Why was he asking me about Barry Manilow right then and there at the ballgame? Had he lost his mind? "He's all right, Dan. Why?" I impatiently replied, trying to focus on the ballgame.

Dan was still standing up. Everyone in our section seemed to be watching the scene play out as he continued loudly and yelled, "I have tickets for Barry Manilow in

Las Vegas on the thirtieth of the month, front row seats, and I want to take you with me." Now more heads turned, eyebrows were raised and every eye was directly upon me.

What did I say? How embarrassing was this moment? I didn't want anyone to think I was interested in that man and I was tired of his antics. "Dan, for God's sake, sit down and shut up," I yelled back his way. "We are all trying to watch the baseball game!"

Oh no. Dan got up and was headed my way, making all those fans between his seat and mine stand up to let him come through. Dan, with his foaming beer and his spit cup. Oh joy. Do you think everyone turned their heads back to watch the game again at that point in time? No way. They were all tuned in at high alert and were interested in what would happen in my seat with this disruptive, unruly, loud, fat lipped, tobacco-chewing, stud wannabe who was headed my direction. All eyes were on us.

Dan sat down in the empty seat next to my girlfriend and leaned over her to talk to me. I had never heard our section as quiet as it was at that moment when Dan began telling me why I needed to join him in Vegas. He wanted me to accompany him to see his all-time favorite performer, Barry Manilow. Naturally, he had the best possible seats at the MGM. He didn't expect me to stay in the same hotel room with him, but he really wanted me to go with him. I did my very best to let him down easy, I truly did. I knew everyone was listening to the little soap opera in Section 114.

"Dan," I said, "I'm not interested in going to Vegas, or seeing Barry Manilow, or anyone else for that matter, with you. And I'd really like it if you could just go back to your seat to watch the rest of the game."

Dan got the last word. He stood up, puffed up his chest, spit in his cup, took a long drink of his foaming beer and said, "You don't know what you're missing, Rose. You are missing out on me and Barry Manilow." And off Dan stumbled towards his seat at the end of the aisle, making everyone stand up again so that he could pass by.

Those friends close to me started giggling and making little comments; it was humorous but humiliating at the same time. I'd like to say that was the end of the night; however, it wasn't. Towards the end of the game, the beer and tobacco evidently got the very best of Dan and he vomited on the concrete between his legs. My girlfriend and I saw it happen and we were mortified. Dan got up, stumbled up the stairs and didn't return. No one in our section could believe the drama of the night and I simply hoped it was over for good. For weeks after that, someone in the section would say, "Hey Rose! Do you like Barry?" and we would all laugh. Unfortunately, to this day, guess who I think of every time I hear a Barry Manilow song? Yup. None other than Dan the Harley Man.

So Dan left me alone after that. I didn't intend for it to end the way it did, but Dan had different plans by reintroducing himself into my life after I bid him farewell. This Frog just didn't want to get off of my lily pad. You may meet Frogs in the future who just simply don't want to let go. If you aren't interested in them, tell them as gently as you can. If saying it in a kind manner doesn't work … well, say it a little stronger. And if all else fails, you may have to tell him to sit down and shut up, and let you and everyone else around you watch the baseball game! Shortly after that unforgettable evening, I noticed Dan started attending the last of that season's ballgames with a female companion who appeared to be interested in Dan and all he had to offer. Hopefully she liked Barry. 🐸

DON'T BELIEVE EVERYTHING THEY SAY, AND AVOID DRAMA NO MATTER WHAT!

I've heard many lies in my lifetime and quite a few of them came from the croaking mouths of several Frogs I met through online dating. I shared with you some of those lies in an earlier chapter. Lying about their height, their age, their marital status. So many lies are told. The problem is that there is absolutely nothing one can do about someone who chooses to lie. I mean, once you discover that what they are sharing is actually a lie, of course you have a choice of whether you continue to see them or not. But since you can't put them on a chair in the corner for it, what else is there to do? There is no online dating Time Out. There should be. Wouldn't it be awesome if one could post a badge or banner on the online dating profile of someone who lies for all to see? Maybe there would be other badges or banners as well. For the lying person, perhaps a depiction of Pinocchio with the very long nose. For someone who is married but presenting themselves as single, perhaps a mangy dog on the banner. These would only be seen by the opposite sex but it would be a way to disqualify those guys who have lied or misled others deliberately. I'm all for equal opportunity, so there would be the same opportunity available for the profiles of women with the same options. Perhaps a banner with a pile of gold and a shovel – yes, for the gold diggers. There are many of them out there as well. I would also like to see a place where one could rate the person they dated on the website. A five-star ranking like they do for hotels, or perhaps something similar to the Rotten Tomatoes website for movies. That would certainly make selecting a potential date easier, wouldn't it?

Of course, no dating website would allow such tomfoolery on their site as it would make their member population nervous. After all, beauty is in the eye of the beholder, and one person's trash is another one's treasure, agreed? I do want to mention the gold diggers for a moment since I referred to them briefly above. Mainly this applies to the women on dating websites who use Frogs to get lunches, dinners or whatever free gifts they are offering. Many of these women don't plan to reciprocate with any gifts of their own. They simply want life to be a little better and expect men to provide for them willingly with no questions asked. Perhaps they are struggling by raising several children on a meager income and can't afford to go out to nice restaurants. I'm certainly not down playing the tough spot some women get put in after divorce. However, having the attitude of letting Frogs pay and pay and continue to pay is not appropriate on any level. Why not let some interested Frog pick up the tab and enjoy the moment with no actual plan to see him again? How do I know this happens? Frogs I met from dating websites eagerly told me so. The main reason they shared this with me was because I offered to pay for my own dinner every date. Typically, no gentleman wanted a woman to pay for him and he usually refused; however, if we had a second date, I paid for it. But believe me, I was a minority in just making the offer (and willing to go through with it) on that first date. If you are on a dating website and have a first date, make the offer to pay for the first dinner or movie or coffee. At least offer to pay for yourself. It makes all the difference in the world. No Frog wants to be viewed as an open checkbook or be taken advantage of.

But back to the subject of a whole new level of lying. The story I am going to share will take the cake on lying. It is so outlandish that all one can do in the end is shake their head and say "Hmmm." It's that over the top, and how this certain guy thought he could make it work still dumbfounds me. I may have had some blonde in my hair, but there were truly no blonde roots. There's a big difference, isn't there? No wonder he ended up with a blonde woman in the very end– at least as long as she could stand him, I'm told.

Tommy was and still is very smooth. When I got his first email through the dating website, he asked me if I had attended a particular baseball game on a recent Friday night. Remember I said I am very recognizable? If someone saw my photos and then saw me out in public, they would remember me. Truth be told, it was my hair – wild colors and one of a kind style. If you have an obvious appearance or are equally as recognizable, the one thing I suggest is to be very careful what profile name you choose online. Since real names are not used on dating websites to protect the privacy of the member, each person picks a "handle," nickname or catch phrase as their profile name. I've seen some interesting ones and some downright stupid ones. For instance, a guy may choose "Big Stud 69" or "He Man." A woman may choose "Loves to Cook" (right) or "Make Me Yours." Whatever the name chosen, just be ready for it to be called out across the aisle of a grocery store. I say this because it happened to me once during those online dating years. Let me share that story and then I'll get back to talking about Tommy – which, by the way, was his favorite subject.

Here is how it went down. I stopped at the local grocery store after work one evening, minding my own business and pushing my cart down the cereal aisle. I was wearing my work clothes, which was typically a dress or skirt and high heels. Out of the blue, a guy walked up to me and said quite loudly, "Hey, Girly Girl?!"

I froze. People in the aisle were now watching us. I stared at the guy standing right in front of me, running through in my head the guys I was currently writing to online to filter through their names, and BAM! I knew who it was. "Ed?" I said as I smiled at him. Oh, the return smile on his face was so wide and wonderful. We had never met, had been writing for a few weeks to each other, and I knew instantly who he was. Luckily for me, I have an uncanny recall of names and faces. Now you see why choosing an appropriate username is so important. Imagine how the people in the store shopping near me would have felt if Ed would have called out, "Hey, Hot Wet Britches?"

But I am off track and I promised to return to my first story. Let's get back to Tommy, the man who I doubt told me one truthful statement on any of our dates. This man recognized me at a baseball game, sent me an email and asked if I had been at that game the Friday night before. "Did you sit in a section behind third base and were you wearing black shorts and a white top?" he asked. He had indeed seen me and, yes, I was impressed. I took some time to review his profile and found him nice looking and interesting. He was not afraid to share how wonderful he was and all the toys he had. I wrote back and we agreed to meet later that week at another baseball game. He invited me to sit next to him in his season ticket seats behind home plate. He said he was smitten and he absolutely had to meet me. I accepted.

As I usually did during the week when I would attend baseball games, I wore whatever my outfit had been at work that day. Again, that is typically a skirt or dress and high heels. I showed up for the game, picked up the ticket he had left for me at Will Call, and made my way to his section and seats. Tommy was waiting for me with two cold beers and a big smile. I will admit that he was very attractive, although not as tall as I typically like guys to be. It's the heels. Remember, I have to add two to five inches to my own height, which means I'm looking in the eyes or down at most guys. No worries. I sat down to have a beer and get to know the mystery man.

The first story Tommy told me was about when he'd seen me the weekend before. "I was with my son," he said. "We were getting something to eat and I happened to look over towards third base and I saw you walking up the aisle. Well, I grabbed my chest and fell against the wall. A policeman came and asked me if I was okay. I said, 'Yes, officer, but the sight of a certain woman in another section almost gave me a heart attack.'" Now you and I both know that this story is a crock of crap; however, hearing Tommy share this with me on our first date was endearing. And he was so sincere – at least I thought so at the time. He made me laugh, and that can be a good sign. Like other guys I had dated, Tommy could talk on and on about what I was realizing was his favorite subject which, as I've said, was Tommy. I'm a good listener and enjoyed the evening anyway.

It didn't take long to eventually confirm that this man was not only not shy about bragging about himself, but he said a lot of things that I wasn't sure were true. Now I realize in all actuality, Tommy had very low self-esteem, so the more he could build himself up, the better he felt. He had lived all his life in a small community down the road from the ballpark and his family name was known in the local area. He had been on the city council in his small town and previously held the position of Fire Chief. That is, until he got sick with cancer and had to devote all his efforts to his health. Now he was completely recovered and focusing his efforts on impressing me. At least for the time being.

After the first date at the baseball game, the following weekend Tommy and I had a dinner date at a very nice restaurant. And guess what! It wasn't a Mexican restaurant. It was very romantic and I must admit I enjoyed it very much. Tommy was extremely complimentary and sweet. He dropped me back off at my house that evening with plans made for me to join him at the next Friday night high school football game in his little town. Friday night games are huge in small communities and everyone attends. He kept telling me all week that everyone who knew him would be there at the game, including both his ex-wives and likely his three kids. He warned that I should be prepared to have people stare at me as they wondered who exactly this "outsider" who was attending the game with him actually was. It was a very cliquish community and they didn't like outsiders, he said. Wow. What year in high school were we in anyway? Really? Okay, I decided I would get my game face on and be prepared for the crowd to yell, "Stranger, go home!" as we entered the stadium. The boo-hiss sounds would be heard for miles and I would likely dodge rotten fruit the whole game.

The reality of the situation was this. No one yelled at me. People stared, but that was most likely because of my hair. Smaller communities typically haven't seen my kind of hairstyle, and it draws a few looks from some rather uptight observers. I get the same looks from those who live in my home state of Montana. I had fun at the football game and Tommy seemed to enjoy the attention as he stopped and spoke to several dozen people on the way to our seats. I stress that Tommy talked to them – Tommy did not introduce me to them. Truly, I think Tommy got the biggest kick out of my being there, as it put him in the spotlight. It wasn't about me at all. It was about Tommy.

Other things I learned about this man during those few short weeks together was that he claimed to own the golf course in his community. He had a little house (previously his mother's) on the golf course and he liked to go cut the grass on his golf course. The truth was that the small house on the road to the golf course was indeed his mother's; however, the golf course was not his. It was a public community course, and while he may have gone to mow the grass, it wasn't because he owned it. He did take me to that house near the course (I had played golf there in my previous married life) and showed me things inside the house. Since his mother had passed away, he owned the house and all its contents, although he lived in a larger house in town. Why he wanted to show me the crystal, the handmade doilies, the antique furniture and other treasures was beyond me. He kept saying that everything was his now, and he just didn't know what he was going to do with all of it. I was not impressed. I realized again that it was all about Tommy.

Another stretch of the truth I remember Tommy telling me was that he had an airport hangar full of antique collectible cars. You know, old restored Cadillacs, BMWs and many more. Some were his and some had been his father's before he passed away. Why would a man share this with a woman he has just met? Wasn't he worried that she would be interested in what he had rather than who he was? During that same drive in his truck (not one of the old cars – he never showed me any of those), he told me that he had three Rolex watches. He was wearing one that day, although I wouldn't know a Rolex from a Timex unless I put my reading glasses on and got close enough to read the fine print. Again, why would he tell me this? He was a light prop plane pilot (this part was true) and he used to have his own plane but sold it. He was looking for another one to buy. I asked myself over and over again – why was he sharing all this with me when he hadn't asked me anything about myself. Yes, it was all about Tommy.

One very good date we had included boating on a local lake along with his young son and my teenage son and his friend. We had a wonderful time, the weather was perfect and Tommy let me and the boys all drive the boat. He treated all of us to dinner afterwards at a quaint country dance hall that had a nice restaurant, and every one of us had a great time. Naturally, my teenage son was quite excited that his mom was dating someone with a boat. There is nothing more exciting for a teenager than the thought of spending many weekends on the lake doing some wake boarding. Too bad it didn't last that long.

I learned a lot about Tommy in those few short weeks, but he didn't seem as interested in me as he was in my getting to know all about him and what he had. I seriously had my doubts already, but later that following week when Tommy called to share some very disturbing news with me, I was even less sure. It was a weeknight and I happened to be home as there was no baseball game that evening. I remember sitting down on a little stool in my kitchen when Tommy started talking. "Rose, I need to share some information with you and I want you to take it very seriously," he said. "I need to know right now if you have anything to hide." My heartbeat increased and I was listening intently. What the heck was this all about? Tommy continued with the reason for his urgent call. It appeared that one of his ex-wives had seen us at the football game (shocking) and she wanted to know who this strange woman was that might be spending time with their young son in the future. According to Tommy, she planned to do a background check on me, and if there were anything at all in my past that could be considered derogatory, she would forbid Tommy to let their son be around me. Tommy continued by asking me if I had ever been convicted of a felony or had a bankruptcy or anything as little as a speeding ticket. Did I need to confess anything to him before she ran the background check and reported the findings to him? I was speechless for about 10 seconds.

"Have you lost your mind? You have some nerve, Tommy. No one can run a background check without knowing personal information about me. How does she intend to do that? What have you been telling her about me?" I said angrily.

"She works for a mortgage company and has access to records in the real estate community," Tommy replied.

I was flabbergasted. I was amazed and not in a good way. I was pissed! Who did this guy think he was to threaten me and make me feel guilty when I had absolutely nothing to hide from him or his ex-wife? This was some kind of special high school drama that I truly didn't need. Drama was something absent in my life. I didn't associate with girlfriends who brought their drama into my life, I avoided drama at work and I kept my very minute drama to myself when it happened. Drama kills relationships, and when a new person entering your life immediately introduces drama or unloads a ton of baggage, things are going to go downhill fast. Ex-spouses can be the biggest instigators of drama in a new relationship, depending on the overall health of the relationship terminating; however, it's much more troublesome when that drama is introduced by the possible Prince Charming himself!

I was quite upset when I hung up the phone with Tommy. At that time I believed what he said and thought his ex-wife was really out to get me. He seemed intent on making me believe that. I was actually distressed about the possibility of having a background check run on me even though I had nothing to hide and knew she really shouldn't have access to my information. It's that same feeling you get when you are pulled over by a policeman. You know you weren't speeding, have no idea why you were pulled over, but you feel guilty and get the shakes nevertheless. I came to realize that Tommy was living in a fantasy world, one where every woman wanted him – including the two ex-Mrs. Tommy's. In this world, he was king. Everyone had to worship the ground he walked on and newcomers to the kingdom were thrown to the lions to test their survival skills. Well, this newcomer was not interested in entering the lion pit nor taking any more particular grief from Tommy, or his loyal subjects or harem. Unfortunately, this battle with the truth was not quite over for me yet. I still had one more phone call to answer in just a few short days.

I hadn't had much conversation with Tommy that week and although I saw him at a baseball game, I didn't sit by him. Instead, I went with my sister and avoided His Majesty. He texted me a lot that week saying he wanted to see me; however, I was very quiet and kept my distance. I had some personal reflecting to do regarding these newest shenanigans and wasn't quite certain what my decision would be. I was still processing the fact that Tommy appeared to be quite egotistical and perhaps a little bit of a narcissist. It didn't take me long to make a final decision the following night.

When my kitchen phone rang the next evening shortly after arriving home from work, I half expected there to be a solicitor on the other end. Perhaps wanting me to take a survey or sell me something I certainly didn't need. Therefore my tone was anything other than friendly when I picked up the receiver. "Hello?" I said as I walked towards the sink.

"Is this Rose?" the female on the other end of the telephone line asked.

"Yes, it is," I replied. "Who's calling?" Here it was and I was certainly not ready for what was to come.

"My name is Becky. You don't know me," the caller said. "But I know about you and I'd like to know why you are dating my fiancé."

Say what? Fiancé? It took me a moment to understand what she had just said. Then it sunk in. "Really? And who, may I ask, is your fiancé?" I inquired. Now, I know you see this coming; however, at that moment standing in my kitchen with a strange woman calling on the other end of my kitchen phone, I wasn't prepared.

"Tommy. I have been dating Tommy for almost a year and he has asked me to marry him. I said yes and now I find out that he has been seeing you over the past several weeks. He said he met you through an online dating website which is where he met me as well. I'm not going to give up on him so I want to ask you to stop seeing him," Becky replied.

I really hadn't seen this one coming. His highness apparently had several ladies in waiting and I, unfortunately, was considered one in that mix. I was still reeling from the thought of having his ex-wife run a background check on me to see if I was 'safe' to be around her son. Now I was talking on the phone with his fiancé? How did this Becky person find out about me, I wondered? I had to ask.

"How do you know I've been seeing Tommy?" I asked her.

Becky explained that she read his texts and got my number from his phone. She said she was willing to fight for him and wanted to give me the opportunity to bow out gracefully. She wasn't going to have to ask me twice. I was so done with Tommy and his drama! But not until I got my say so.

"You do realize that Tommy has been passing himself off as completely single and available, don't you?" I asked. "If he's proposed to you, why has he been seeing me and continuing to plead for me to keep doing so? At best, he is a two-timer. Perhaps there are even more of us. Does this even matter to you? Why would you want to build a future with a man who is clearly not faithful or committed to you? I had already made my decision to stop seeing Tommy because I found him to be a liar and deceitful. Haven't you had the same experience with him?"

"I am going to marry him," she replied.

I wished her good luck, asked her not to contact me again and hung up. Then I texted Tommy to tell him his fiancé Becky had contacted me, and that he could kiss my drama-free single ass.

This story doesn't end with that phone call as I did continue to see Tommy at baseball games over the years, from across the five sections that separated our seats. I would sit with my sister or girlfriend behind third base. Tommy would sit behind home plate with his big, blonde buxom new wife Becky. At least for the few years they remained happily married – or at least while they were still living together. Tommy started texting me a few years later when he'd see me at a game, and usually those texts contained one word: "Sigh." Tommy was now sitting behind home plate. Alone.

We've continued to have periodic contact over the years, which typically revolves around Tommy remarking that he should never have let me get away and always being very sweet to me. His texts make me smile, and although I do not condone how he treated me when we first met, I believe in my heart that Tommy wanted to be a good Frog. He simply had trouble separating fantasy from reality and believed the world revolved around – yes, you guessed it. It certainly was and always will be … all about Tommy.

When a Frog enters your life and is more interested in himself than he is in you, move on. If the only thing he cares about is making himself sound fantastic but has no interest in getting to know anything about you, throw him back. If drama enters the picture as a crazy ex-wife or a future wife, leave the area in a big hurry and start kissing Frogs in a new pond. You deserve to be treated with respect. A man should want to know everything there is about you, including your shoe size and what your favorite movie is. Anything less than that is simply unacceptable. Not now. Not ever. 🐸

SOME FROGS IN THE DATING POND AREN'T JUST TOADS – THEY HAVE WARTS

There are Frogs swimming in the online dating pond who are there for their own purposes. Some reasons may not be all good. Previously I mentioned the married men and women passing themselves off as single when in all reality they weren't 100 percent available. Unfortunately, the hopeful person of interest on the other end doesn't realize this until it's too late. By then there are wasted hours, days, weeks or months, and most assuredly some very hurt feelings. Take the story of Laura, one of my girlfriends who tried online dating very briefly. While it didn't end well, it could have been much worse. You be the judge.

Laura typically didn't like online dating but she knew I was meeting some fairly decent guys on a particular website, so she decided to try it. It wasn't long before she met a Frog that she was interested in. They talked on the phone a lot and texted daily for several weeks. They met at a park and talked one afternoon. Things were going very well and she was becoming quite interested in him. Laura invited him over to her house one Sunday afternoon to watch a movie and relax. He accepted and that's exactly what they were doing – watching a movie and sitting on the couch when her front doorbell rang. Ding dong. Followed by a few insistent knocks. Rap, rap, rap.

My friend got up from the couch, went to the front door and opened it to find a woman standing on her front porch. "Yes, may I help you?" Laura said to the stranger looking intently back at her.

"Is my husband here?" said the woman on the porch.

"Who is your husband?" Laura asked.

"Andre," the woman replied.

And being that Andre's truck was in my girlfriend's driveway and he was inside her house, sitting on the couch watching Laura's movie on her TV ... Laura did what most of us would do. She opened up her front door as wide as she could, motioned towards the living room and stood back to watch the fireworks. Mrs. Andre marched into the living room, had some choice loud words to say, and marched right back out with Andre in tow. He was never to be heard from again and my girlfriend avoided online dating sites for a very long time after that very uncomfortable experience.

How did the very clever Mrs. Andre find her cheating, lying husband who presented himself as single on a dating website? She got a hold of his phone, looked up Laura's number online, which also gave her address. Then she waited until she drove by and found her cheating husband's truck parked in that driveway. It was patience that brought Mrs. Andre to the front door and it was a lying, cheating Toad who represented himself as single in the online dating pond that got him inside that door. This Toad not only had warts, he had balls. Big hairy ones.

I had my own experience with a Toad who had warts as well, but I never had a wife show up on my doorstep asking for her husband. My story takes a little turn to an even darker part of humanity and revolves around a particularly nasty Toad with a pretty ugly past. This Toad had some serious nerve and even more serious problems.

Unfortunately, I was exposed to him without realizing exactly how ugly things were.

Rodney was handsome in his own boy next door, intellectual way. Tall, curly dark hair, glasses and a nice smile. We communicated for several weeks and finally met face to face at a country bar where we girls liked to go dancing on Friday nights. Rodney knew I had planned to be out there dancing that particular evening but he didn't say he was joining us. Imagine my surprise when I looked over towards the edge of the dance floor as I passed by with my partner to see Rodney standing there smiling and looking back at me. We recognized each other right away and there was a definite spark. After the song ended, I walked over to him and said hello, we talked for just a few short minutes and as the next song started, he led me onto the floor for our first dance together. And could he dance! We twirled and two stepped around the floor but when the song ended, he said he really needed to go. Naturally, I didn't want him to leave but he was insistent and said he would call me the following day. I thought it quite odd that he popped in for just 10 minutes and left in such a hurry, but I would find out soon enough why that was.

A few days later, Rodney and I had our first real date. Nothing spectacular – a late afternoon lunch date where we talked a lot more and began learning about each other. At least I thought we were. We were both divorced, he was a small business owner, had several kids of varying ages and he had a boat. He said he got to see his kids a few weekends a month but not as much as he would have liked to, even though they lived in the area. My thought was that it must have been a very nasty divorce, as it sounded like he didn't get to spend much time with his kids.

Rodney came over to my house during our next date to pick me up and he seemed a little uncomfortable in my personal space. I should explain that my house is very neat, orderly and I have a tendency to be a closet O.C.D. freak. Okay, maybe not so much in the closet – I probably hang it right out there in plain sight. One thing being such a perfectionist allows for is the ability to notice if anything was moved in my house. And I mean anything. On this particular day, I ran upstairs to my bedroom to grab my shoes and when I came back downstairs, we left on our little outing. It wasn't until Rodney dropped me back off at home that evening that I noticed things were moved around in my kitchen. The salt and pepper shakers had been put up on the windowsill, my counter clock was turned around backwards and I found my potholders in the refrigerator. I was dumbfounded. Why had he messed with my stuff?

I looked in my half bathroom just off the kitchen and found things moved around in that room as well. The hand towel was in the sink rather than hanging on the towel rack. The toilet seat was up rather than down. Water was splashed all over my mirror. Why? What would possess someone to do this? The same for items in my living room – he had moved around my candlesticks that were above the fireplace and knocked my pillows down on the couch. What was he thinking and where was the respect for someone else's personal space? Thank goodness he didn't have more time alone downstairs or he'd have moved everything in my house. My couch would have probably been out on the patio! It didn't make sense to me why Rodney would deliberately mess up my house until I had the chance a few days later to see his house. If you could legally classify it as a house.

Before my trip out to see Rodney's house and meet his kids, I introduced him to my teenage son. We met Rodney at a restaurant and had lunch together. They talked about sports and boating and guy stuff. They hit it off very well and I was quite thrilled to see that. When a woman meets a guy, there is nothing quite as thrilling as watching her own child or children get along very well with that potential Prince Charming. Life is always better in the castle when all residents get along.

I still hadn't addressed his moving stuff in my castle, but figured I'd have plenty of time to inquire as to his little game playing at a later date. One thing I didn't care for immediately with Rodney was that he said I shouldn't wear makeup or lipstick. He said that he would like me to be more natural. He would even lean over the table and try to rub off my lipstick with his napkin. I told him I was girly, I liked wearing makeup and that wasn't going to change. It seemed odd to me that he persisted with bringing up this subject as my photos on my profile clearly showed that I wore makeup and my profile name was "Girly Girl," after all. It was just odd that he seemed to not like several things about me but continued to want to see me.

Not long after, Rodney took me by his ex-wife's house one weekend to meet his kids. We sat outside on a big porch and they each came out to hug him and say hello – except for his oldest daughter. She came out on the porch but stayed close to her mom rather than coming over to greet her dad. He had three girls and one boy. They ranged in ages from about five to 15 years old. He had a very pretty young teenage daughter (the one who wouldn't come hug him) and a moody, sullen older teenage boy, along with two adorable younger daughters. Rodney seemed very loving and warm – his two youngest girls climbed all over his lap and were very happy to see him. His ex-wife stood out on the porch with us the entire time and observed the interaction. I was curious about all of this but didn't give it too much thought. I wanted to spend more time alone with Rodney and we had plans to spend the afternoon together. I did enjoy meeting his kids but thought it strange that we went to their mother's house to do so. I was sure there was a good explanation.

When we left his kids that afternoon, Rodney wanted to stop by his house for a few moments. It was out in a rural area but not too far from his ex-wife's house. When we pulled into his driveway, I wondered if the house was in the process of being torn down. There were actually small holes in the side of the house which were large enough to see through, and it was in desperate need of paint, wood, glass, tar paper and much more. It would have been easier to burn it down and rebuild it than to make it livable. I did my best to not show my shock but when we walked inside; I was truly not prepared. What a dump!

To say that Rodney wasn't the cleanest, most organized single man would be an understatement. The house had more cobwebs hanging inside it than any Halloween haunted house I've ever entered. It reminded me of a long abandoned neighbor's house that my mom took my siblings and me to way out in the country when we were in high school. We called it the Pig Farmer's House because the owners had raised pigs on the property, and one day many years before, they had just up and moved. No one knew exactly where they went, but they were gone. They didn't take much with them when they left, including the pigs, and what was in the house was mainly all over the floors. Once domesticated but now wild pigs had made their way inside the house and destroyed much of what was left behind. Spider webs and hornets' nests were everywhere. Mom, who loved an adventure, took us there to look around in order to salvage anything we could, but I was mortified by the disgusting mess. This was exactly how I felt when I walked inside Rodney's nasty, dilapidated house. I didn't touch anything and kept looking around for spiders and bugs. How could he actually stay in that absolutely unbelievable mess?

We didn't stay long at Rodney's house, which I didn't mind at all. We had a late lunch and he dropped me back off at home. I was never so glad to return to my very clean, organized and near perfect home later that afternoon. Thoughts went through my mind about where we would live if our relationship ever came to that point of togetherness. God knows I couldn't spend a day in that mess, let alone live there. It was truly a structure that should have had a sign on the door stating it was condemned. And he lived there! No wonder he felt he had to move items in my house. Perhaps he just didn't feel comfortable with such simplicity and order. Unfortunately, this was not the worst part of Rodney – that part was waiting for me just on the other side of the next lily pad.

But before I learned of that ugly part of Rodney, I had my own nasty experience while spending time with him that ultimately became one of the freakiest, frightful happenings in my entire life.

The Saturday started out wonderfully with plans to take Rodney's boat out to the lake. My son and his friend joined us and they were both very excited to do some wake boarding. Rodney picked us up at my house that morning with his boat in tow, and off we went to a local lake to spend the day.

Once we arrived at the lake, Rodney began unloading the boat into the water and suggested that anyone who needed to use the restroom take advantage of doing so before we headed out on the water. As I entered the women's restroom, I was deep in thought wondering why none of Rodney's kids were joining us to go boating. It would have been fun to have his teenagers join us so that they could spend some time with my son. I hadn't asked Rodney why he hadn't invited them but decided I would do so later that afternoon. My mind was distracted with these thoughts as I entered my stall, pulled down my swimsuit bottoms and began to do my business.

It was while sitting on the toilet that I noticed several big daddy longlegs spiders on the wall on both sides of me. They were the biggest spiders I had ever seen. Texas sized. I carefully got some toilet paper off the roll and sat there quietly hoping not to disturb them. Spiders can jump and I was not in a hurry to have any of them join me on the toilet. A couple of the spiders began moving around on the wall and I began getting a little edgy. I may as well tell you that I don't like spiders at all. And even though daddy longlegs don't bite, or so I've been told, they brought back unpleasant memories. While visiting our grandmother when we were kids, my cousin used to pull the legs off of these types of spiders and throw the big, fat bodies at my sisters and me. They just freaked me out.

It was with that thought resting uneasily on my mind that I decided to eliminate those few spiders that were closest to me on the wall. I reached down carefully and removed my flip flop. Aiming carefully, I smacked the one nearest me on the right side of the wall. Smack! I felt a little bit better knowing that was one less spider hovering near me. Daddy longlegs can not only jump, but they are fast; I was so not interested in playing that little game with these ugly creatures. 'May as well take a few more out while I'm still sitting on the toilet doing my business,' I thought. Smack! There went one on the left side of the wall. Rose – 2, Spiders – 0.

And then I felt it. Something was crawling on the side of my thighs, hips and buttock. On both sides of my thighs, hips and buttock, actually. I forgot the spiders lurking on the walls and looked down. I couldn't even immediately process what I was seeing. Climbing up over my thighs, over my hips and onto the tops of both of my legs were a black mass of daddy longlegs. There were at least 20 of them coming up from underneath the toilet and making their way up over my exposed, naked thighs, hips and buttock. I freaked the hell out.

I came off that toilet seat with a blood-curdling scream

and exited the bathroom stall in one huge frantic leap. While beating the spiders that were on my legs off with my wildly swinging arms and using the one flip flop still in my right hand, I continued to scream at the top of my lungs. The stall door slammed loudly shut and I began dancing around the floor like a mad woman. My swimsuit bottoms were down around my ankles, I kept screaming and had the biggest case of the heebie-jeebies I'd ever experienced in my entire life. And I believe I finished going pee right there on the floor while I stood outside that bathroom stall screaming.

I finally got myself together and calmed down. Checking to be sure there were no more spiders still crawling on me, I finally pulled up my swimsuit bottoms and opened up the bathroom stall again. I simply had to see what in the world happened in there! I bent over to see the area closest to the floor. Underneath the toilet was a solid black mass of daddy longlegs spiders. The white toilet was absolutely black underneath with a writhing, moving glob of spiders, and they were still crawling up and over the toilet seat. I had three stalls to choose from when I entered the bathroom and I had picked the one that a huge nest of spiders decided to build their home under to sit upon. And while doing so, killed two of their relatives who were on the wall minding their own business while I was taking care of mine. They certainly got their revenge, though. Rose – 2, Spiders – 1,000.

I left the bathroom in a very big hurry and ran right smack into my son, his friend and Rodney. They had heard my screams and thought I was being murdered in the ladies restroom. I shared with them what had happened and they all had a nice laugh. I was not amused and kept thinking of those spiders throughout the afternoon. It should have been a premonition of things to come as all was not to be exactly right with continuing to get to know Rodney, and it would turn just as ugly as that black mass of spiders under the toilet.

A few days after that awful outing with the spiders, Rodney called me on the phone one weeknight to talk. He was just leaving a meeting he had attended and said he needed to share something with me. We had hit it off very well up to this point (except his disgusting, dilapidated house, his need to redecorate mine and the experience with the spiders) and before we got serious about each other, he said there was something I needed to know. He very suddenly had my full attention and to this day, I can recall clearly standing in my combination office-workout room upstairs listening to what he had to share with me that evening. Rodney had just left an evening therapy group (did he say therapy?) and the other members of this group had asked him repeatedly over the past few weeks if he had told me his story. Who has a story that a therapy group asks if you've shared? Whatever it was, they were adamant that he share it with me so that I could decide if I wanted to continue to be involved in his life. He owed me that much, is what they said to him earlier and he repeated to me on the phone that night. Whoa. This had gone to a whole new level of What the Hell? I wasn't even aware that Rodney went to a therapy group.

As I sat down on the closet floor (I had been getting ready to file papers in the filing cabinet in the closet), I said to Rodney, "I'm all ears." And I was. If I had known how very ugly the conversation was going to be and the fact that I would be sick to my stomach for days after, I'd have likely just disconnected the line and gone on my happy way. But we don't expect that these Frogs we kiss can actually be Toads and that some of those Toads will have warts that will leave a scar where they touch you. Forever. Rodney began by saying that he really liked me and he hoped that what he had to tell me wouldn't immediately influence me to stop seeing him. He wanted me to listen to all that he had to share and then take some time to decide how I felt and how I wanted to move forward. I agreed that I would do so. I mean, how bad could it be? I had already lived through the spider ordeal.

His story went something like this – he was attending a therapy group and was being held accountable by other members in that group to be honest, factual and upfront about who he was. When he shared with the members of this group that he had started seeing me, they asked him, "Does she know?" They stressed their expectation for him to come clean and that's why he needed to have this conversation with me that night as he was driving home. He had committed to the group to tell me the truth immediately; however, I found out later through a mutual acquaintance that Rodney downplayed some of the ugliness in this particular story. It's my belief that Rodney didn't tell me the whole story whatsoever. It is certainly ugly enough as told that evening, but I will let you be the judge.

The night Rodney met me in the country dance club, he said I probably noticed that he was a little nervous and may have wondered why he had to leave so quickly after arriving. I told him, yes – I remembered that very clearly. He also asked if I had wondered why he never had his kids for the whole weekend, why they didn't join us boating and why he went to see them at his ex-wife's house. Yes, I also agreed that I had wondered that as well. The reason for not staying at the dance club was that he was not allowed to be in any establishment whatsoever that served alcohol. This was a result of currently being on probation. When he said this, I waited. Pure silence. I was not going to ask what the probation was for and make it easy on him. If he needed to confess, he was going to have to do it like a man.

Rodney continued by saying he was not allowed to be alone with any of his children unsupervised – it required court approved supervision, to be exact. What? I wondered very briefly before Rodney continued talking what he could have possibly done to only be allowed to see his kids with court approved supervision. In fact, he stated, he couldn't be around any children under the age of 18 at all unless he was supervised. Wait, what? My son and his friend were under 18 years old and he certainly was around them for a whole day boating. Wow, this was going quickly from bad to worse. The reason for all this supervision and court appointed control, Rodney told me, was because he was a convicted child molester. My body went cold and I felt my dinner leaving my stomach and rushing at full force towards my throat. A convicted child molester! When? How? Who? Why? This is a Frog that I had kissed, had intimate thoughts about and fantasies that perhaps he was the Prince Charming I had been looking for. Did he just tell me that he was a convicted child molester? A child molester?! Yes, it appeared that is exactly what he had just told me. WTF? I was going to throw up. I repeat – WTF or as we said in the military, Whiskey Tango Foxtrot!

Rodney then shared that part of this uncomfortable confession required by his therapy group was that I was allowed to ask questions of him. Any question I wanted to ask him. He was held accountable by his peers (now this therapy thing made sense) to let me inquire to my heart's content. I took a deep breath and began my inquisition. "When did this happen, Rodney?"

"It was about two years ago," he replied. "I spent some time in jail, got an attorney and now I'm on probation."

I never did find out if his probationary period was forever or for a term of some number of years. I do know, however, that he is currently listed on the registered sex offender website (yes, I checked) and is required to update his address every time he moves. You have certainly heard of the type. Any interested or curious person can go look online to search for a convicted sex offender in the neighborhood that they live in or plan to move into so they can identify any sex offenders living nearby. We all want to keep our children safe, right? Well, no wonder Rodney lived out in the country in that piece of crap, dilapidated, dump of a house. Who would want to be his neighbor?

I continued with my questioning even as my throat started to constrict and my dinner continued to push against that little bobbing thing that hangs down at the back of my tongue. It was hard to even ask the next question because I wasn't sure I wanted to know. But I had to know. I truly did. I asked him, "Who with, Rodney?" I wasn't prepared to hear the answer but it came rolling across the phone waves and nestled nastily into my ear for my brain to digest. Rodney then speaks the name of his oldest daughter. His teenage daughter, yes. His own flesh and blood. What in God's name? Now it made more sense that she was not interested in greeting him at her mom's house and was reserved. I knew Rodney was hoping I wouldn't ask the next question, but I had to. I needed to know exactly what we were talking about here, and although I did find out later that he likely downplayed this part, his answer was convincing enough for me to know that this particular Frog was not what he seemed. He was actually a Toad, and one that had ugly, disgusting warts all over his body. My skin began to crawl.

"How did this happen? What actually happened?" I asked with an uncanny amount of self-control as serious emotional waves of despair passed over me.

"You really want to know what I did?" he asked me then.

I paused. What? He was questioning me and trying to make me feel guilty? Yes, I certainly did want to know what happened and I didn't even care that it was clearly uncomfortable for him to have to share this with me. Why was he trying to make me feel like the bad guy for asking this question? I was not the convicted child molester here. I believed I had a right to know at that point. I was absolutely certain that the story he shared with me was not the whole truth and nothing but the truth, so help me, God. Please take your seats. Thank you, Your Honor. However, this is what he told me.

Rodney was watching TV in his bed when his young

teenage daughter came in to cuddle and watch some evening program with him. Just the two of them alone. She was in her pajamas and he was in his boxers. Apparently they were under the covers and some extremely inappropriate touching went on. He was fondling his young teenage daughter intimately in his bed with hardly any clothes on – or so his story went. But he didn't get an erection, he said. Oh? I was not buying it, and rightfully so. As the story continued, a few days later the young daughter told her mother what happened in the bedroom with her father. The mother naturally freaked, like any of us would do, and called the police, and the rest became legal history. Rodney was arrested, jailed and eventually convicted, although not imprisoned as his daughter decided not to testify. Now he couldn't see his children without a state approved chaperone (which his ex-wife happened to be), he was not allowed to be in any drinking establishment, had to avoid places where children were, was not to have access to any computer and was listed on the state's convicted sex offender website for life.

Wait one cotton-picking moment. I had met this man online through a dating website. He had been ordered by the state to not have any access, absolutely none, to any computers, and he was on a dating website? He was also not allowed to be in any establishment that served alcohol but he disobeyed those rules and came into that country dance club to meet me. Additionally, he was forbidden to have unauthorized, unsupervised contact with any person under the age of 18, but he had joined my young teenage son and me for lunch and had taken us boating! Did he believe that rules didn't apply to him? Apparently so. Real men do not molest their daughters. I was trying to soak all this in and I still couldn't grasp the gravity of what he had done.

"Will you give this some thought before making a decision about me, Rose? Please let me know when you can if you will agree to continue to see me again," he said.

I explained that I had more questions, to which he replied that he'd be willing to answer at a later date. He believed we had covered enough for one night. I agreed to give it some thought and said we could talk in a few days. I hung up the phone feeling very dirty with the realization that I now needed to have a conversation with my son. I was feeling too many emotions at that point in time. I sat on the floor of my closet, looking at the wall and wondering how in the holy hell I had gotten myself into this predicament. I was trying to recall what Rodney's online profile had said and wished that I could read again what he had put on the dating website. How had I missed that this guy was not who I thought he was? Shortly after we met, Rodney removed his profile from the dating website. He said he was tired of being on there and was truly interested in me; however, now I knew exactly why he had deleted it. Because he wasn't supposed to be on the computer, or any website at all!

The next evening I had a talk with my son and told him what had happened with my conversation and discovery the night before. I shared all of what I had learned and asked him what he thought of our continuing with Rodney. The reason I asked my son what he thought was because whomever I brought into my life would also be in his life. My son didn't have the right to make the final decision but he certainly had the right to give input. He was shocked, appalled and even asked me, "How could someone do that, Mom?" I had no answer for him. I personally had no understanding of how a father could molest his own daughter and then believe he was above the law. I knew in my heart that I was finished with Rodney, but my son's question confirmed that decision tenfold.

I emailed Rodney later that night to let him know that my son and I had decided that we would not allow his type of ugliness into our life. We had to protect our family, as that was so much more important. If Rodney had been honest, I would have never met him. If Rodney had followed the rules imposed legally on him by the state, he would not have been on that dating website at all. If Rodney had been a Frog instead of a Toad – with big fat, ugly, pus-filled warts, I wouldn't be writing this chapter. The really awful part is that Rodney hurt his family, traumatized his daughter and left a nasty scar on me. And to make matters worse, he downplayed his physical involvement with his young teenage daughter. He didn't just fondle her. Rodney, this disgusting specimen of a man, had sex with his own daughter. It's very sad that he wasn't sent to federal prison for what he did. He got off easy with time served and probation. I don't think he took any part of his punishment seriously. He simply didn't deserve to be free, out in public, lying and doing things he wasn't supposed to be doing. Like meeting me and changing my life forever.

There are a lot of wonderful Frogs on the many online dating websites. Decent, honest, respectable, hardworking, polite Frogs who are just waiting for their Princess to bend down and kiss them as they swim along in the water. Unfortunately, there are Toads mixed in that pond, and hiding down in the depths beneath the lily pads lurk those Toads like Rodney who have warts. Keep your eyes open and learn to discern the difference. Question things when they don't seem right. Listen to your intuition. Be picky. And when a wart-infested Toad surfaces in your pond, grab him by the throat and throw that sucker back as far and hard as you can (because you simply can't drown them)! And always check under outdoor public toilets for dark things hiding and crawling there as well. One simply can't be too careful. 🐸

CHOOSE TO BE KIND TO NON-KEEPERS

The experience that a Frog has with others during their online happenstances will mold and shape his impressions for all future dates with other women. Likewise, you either have or will form your beliefs for future dates around those that you meet. It is with that thought in mind that I chose to be kind to those Frogs I knew upon first kiss were not my Prince Charming. If they were kind to me, I returned the kindness. Even if it wasn't my first reaction.

Damon was one of those Frogs. Again, had I listened to my intuition when looking at his profile photos, I may have decided against meeting him. He had two photos. Both were taken from a distance and, yes, he was wearing sunglasses and a hat. Sound familiar? I'd already been down this road and my intuition was screaming loudly that things weren't all that they seemed to be. What caused me to meet Damon in person when I had doubts? Our phone conversations. We spent the better part of a week talking for hours on the phone. I would lie on my white leather couch, upside down with my legs up on the wall. I'd giggle. He'd laugh. We shared so many of our online dating experiences, our upbringing, our goals – we clicked. We made plans for our first date.

My first thought when arriving at the sushi restaurant that Saturday night was the hope of not being disappointed as I had been so many times before. As I pulled into the parking spot, I could see Damon across the parking lot leaning against his truck. Yes, I knew he had been in a bad skiing accident when he was a teenager. This left him with one leg shorter than the other. But seeing him in the same clothing as his photos (jeans, tennis shoes, T-shirt and a ball cap) for our first date, this was disappointing. As I exited my vehicle and walked towards Damon, I did feel some slight despair. He was clearly not my type. He certainly was not my Prince Charming. There would be no spark, no kiss and no second date. But at that very moment, as I moved towards Damon, I made the conscious decision to be kind. To be gracious and full of sweetness when many women wouldn't have been. As we entered the restaurant, I told myself to pretend I was having dinner with the Damon on the phone – not the Damon sitting in front of me. I would treat this man sharing my little table as we kneeled without our shoes on with great kindness. I would remember the laughs, the stories and the fun from the phone conversations. I would reach back into those memories and enjoy the moment. I would not become the ugly, unkind woman in one of those stories that would be told to others in the future. I would be kind.

That is what I did. I enjoyed the evening with Damon. We laughed, we giggled and we had a very enjoyable dinner. Damon was extremely complimentary, he was sweet and he was kind. He said he knew he was not actually my type and that he held no hopes that we would continue to date. This past week of getting to know each other had meant everything to him and he thanked me for being gracious and kind. It restored his confidence and belief in the online dating experience when he was very close to giving up. For that, he said, he would be forever grateful.

Yes, I went away from that evening feeling disappointed as I had invested time in a possible relationship that didn't turn out to be what I expected. But isn't that necessary in all things? We have to invest the time and effort in order to reap the rewards. Nothing comes easily or for free. I didn't continue to share time on the phone with Damon; however, my memory of what we did invest in each other is a good one. I can be pleased with how I treated him in the end. Furthermore, I left him with a good experience that would hopefully open his heart to find his Princess.

There were other Frogs in my pond that turned out not to be my Prince Charming but were overall very good experiences. Again, kindness prevails. One of the sweetest Frogs I've ever kissed that wasn't my Prince Charming but became a wonderful friend was Emilio. We spent the better part of a Christmas holiday exchanging emails and getting to know each other online. He made it clear that he was seeing someone, but the relationship was new so he hadn't taken his profile off the dating website yet. I knew that Emilio wasn't my type, but I found him to be sweet and funny. I enjoyed getting to know him.

I entertained Emilio one evening over the holidays by taking photos of my feet in several of my hooker heels and emailing them to him. At that time, I had an entire room devoted to just shoes and he found it fascinating. He would ask if I had a certain color or style of shoes, I would go get them and take a picture. With a whole room full of shoes, I had a lot to choose from and it made him happy. I mean, he was a hot blooded guy, so why wouldn't he enjoy getting photos of sexy shoes attached to a woman's feet? He didn't have to know that I was in my pajamas in the unseen top of the photo and that I didn't have any makeup on. I was a complete mess. Even so, I thoroughly enjoyed our time together that evening as a single girl can be extremely lonely in the evenings over the holidays. Emilio brought laughter, fun and friendship to me that night. I was very much interested in meeting him.

We made a date to meet for lunch on New Year's Eve. I was getting off work at noon and was looking forward to spending time with him. I let him know that I wasn't dressed up so he shouldn't expect too much – I was very casual. When I entered the restaurant, there was Emilio. He looked just like his photo and after we introduced ourselves, he said, "Wow. You really are dressed casual!" I think he may have been expecting to see me in a pair of those high heels with the rest of the package to match. It made me laugh. It was kind of cute that he was so disappointed in my being dressed down without heels.

Emilio and I continued to share lunches together for several years. He was the guy I called to have lunch with the day my mom passed away. He was endearing, sweet and a good friend. He joined a large part of my family on a trip to Las Vegas for my fiftieth birthday party and everyone loved him. To this day, he calls me his Goddess and I call him Sugar. He wasn't my Prince Charming but he is surely a very sweet and wonderful man who I am fortunate to have met online and continue to know.

Another example of being kind would be my experience with meeting Darren. He was a very eccentric but attractive man who really knew how to dance. I met

Darren online and agreed after a time to meet him out dancing one evening. He said he would be in the Country Room of the same club where Farad met his fateful end. I was with my girlfriend, as we girls tended to travel in pairs when meeting a strange guy out at night. (This is a good idea, by the way, and should be considered for some first meetings with people you don't know.) It wasn't really a "date" – more like a "get acquainted and meet in person" date. If we liked each other, we would then agree to have a real date. I should have stopped before the first date, but one never knows what the future brings.

As I have said before, I am easily recognizable so it wasn't any surprise that I was spotted as soon as we entered the club. Darren smiled and waved when he saw my girlfriend and I enter the Country Room; however, he was out on the dance floor and continued dancing with his partner. Around and around the dance floor they went. Every time they passed us, he would make some silly face or twirl the girl wildly in front of us. It was odd to see, but we were entertained by his antics. Finally, Darren came off the dance floor after many songs and strolled over to us after getting himself a drink. He was a funny and peculiar character, sometimes quite feminine and odd. He would hold his drink in one hand with one pinkie in the air and hold the straw with the other fingers. I was amused if not entirely interested. We chatted for a little bit and then off he went to dance with another girl. I half expected Darren would ask me to dance, but he never did. My girlfriend and I walked into some of the other rooms and danced for a bit. Shortly after, there was Darren standing next to us asking us why we had left the Country Room. I told him we weren't there to be his audience. I wasn't interested in standing around. Secretly, I knew why he never asked me to dance that night. He wasn't convinced I knew how to two-step, waltz or polka. The truth is that I did. Darren was a very good dancer, kind of a show off, and he would never stoop so low as to dance with someone who might step on his shiny boots. He never asked me to dance that night and by the time we did dance together, I was no longer interested in him. By that time, my code name for Darren was P.I.T.A. (Pain in the Ass). But I'm getting ahead of myself. There actually was one real date between us.

Even though my feelings were hurt that Darren didn't want to dance with me at the club the first time we met, I wasn't convinced he was a total loser. However, I wasn't convinced I was attracted to him either. He was tall and very skinny, wore his jeans tighter than any guy I've ever seen and wore the brightest pink or red shirts. Combine that with the upraised pinky drinking cranberry juice routine, it crossed my mind that maybe he was a bit too feminine for my tastes. But one thing I will say for Darren, he was relentless in his pursuit of asking me for a date. He would not quit! I would try to put him off by saying I was busy, I told him I was hurt that he didn't ask me to dance the first time we met, I made up all kinds of excuses, but he wasn't going to shut up until I said yes. He was using up my cell phone's monthly text allowance in the span of one week with his constant begging and pleading for a date. So finally, in a weak moment, I acquiesced and agreed to go to dinner with him. We would meet at a favorite Mexican restaurant of mine because a margarita was surely going to be part of this date, and we would see what the night brought.

It was a Saturday evening and I was tempted all day to cancel the date. However, I knew if I did, Darren would blow my phone up with texts and calls until doomsday. Better to just bite the proverbial bullet and go on the date. I drove to the restaurant with mixed emotions but not real excitement. That should have told me that my heart wasn't in it. When I parked my car, I saw Darren across the parking lot getting out of his truck. Then he was walking towards me in his starched jeans and neon pink shirt with a huge, bright pink bouquet of a dozen long stemmed roses. Not just one single rose. No, an absolute gigantic bunch of roses that he had to hold over his arm so they wouldn't drag on the ground! Wasn't that sweet? Wasn't he the thoughtful one? No. Because Darren didn't want me to put them in my car; he expected me to take them into the restaurant with us!

So, there we went, walking into the restaurant to have dinner and there I was, holding the long stemmed roses over the crook of my arm as Darren held my other arm in his. As we walked up to the hostess to ask for a table, of course she gushed over the long stemmed pink roses I held in my arm.

"Oh, isn't that so sweet? Isn't he so romantic!" she exclaimed. "Aren't you the luckiest girl in the whole wide world?"

I wanted to turn around and go right back out to my car. No, not to put the long stemmed roses in the backseat. I wanted to get back into my car, drive myself home and spend the night on my couch. Alone. But I was way too far past the point of retreat, so I decide to suck it up, buttercup, and get the evening over with. Darren was quite pleased with himself and was grinning from ear to ear. And then he did it. As we entered the dining room full of people eating and drinking and minding their own business, Darren decided it was time to sing. Out loud. Now you have to picture this. He cleared his throat, let me walk a little bit in front of him as we entered the room, and then began to sing. Loudly.

"There she is, Miss America," he sang out clearly for all to hear as I entered the room with the pink, long stemmed roses draped over my arm. Heads turned, conversations stopped, people stared. Darren's smile was bigger than a Cheshire cat's while he escorted me to the table our hostess was leading us to. I was dying. I wanted to slug him. I wanted to trip and fall and require an ambulance immediately. I wanted to gush blood so all of the customers in that part of the dining room would want to leave screaming, gagging and gasping. I wanted the EMS techs (who are usually gorgeous – because they wear uniforms and drive an ambulance) to take me away to the hospital for stitches while Darren stayed behind to remove the long stemmed roses off the floor and be escorted off the premises. Only then could I have been saved this embarrassment of the singing, funny man Darren as he shined a spotlight on the two of us. Sigh. Really? Who does that? He was so proud of himself, while I was absolutely mortified.

Darren pulled out my chair like a true gentleman should and we sat down at the table while I tried to balance the stupid roses on the table without spilling something. I ordered and quickly drank a margarita (a strong one, thank you, Jesus) while Darren sipped on his iced tea with his pinkie finger proudly displayed for all to see. Oh, yes. This man was so pleased with himself and he sat up straight and tall for all to see. He was dining with Miss America and she had the long stemmed roses to prove that fact. The only thing I was missing was the crown. Dinner crawled on, I drank more than I ate and regretfully sat there listening to this man. He was very engaged in conversation during our dinner because he did have a favorite subject he liked to share. Yes, of course – Darren.

The dinner ended and we were ready to go, so I grudgingly picked up the roses and placed them over my arm again to leave the restaurant. I had the fist in my opposite hand clenched tightly in preparation to haul off and knock the holy hell out of Darren if he even began to sing one note of another verse of that cursed song. I didn't even know if there was another verse but, so help me God, I would beat the dog crap out of this man. He didn't say a peep as we exited, so he was saved from the humiliation of being slugged by Miss America in front of everyone in the restaurant. We made it out to the parking lot, he hugged me goodbye and told me that he looked forward to many more dates in our bright future together. I smiled and nodded. 'That's not happening,' I thought.

Needless to say, Darren and I only had one date. Yes, the date where I was Miss America and he was Bert Parks singing the theme song loudly for all to hear. That doesn't mean that Darren didn't ask me for another date. He did. I simply said no, I didn't have time, or I was washing my car or I had a yard to mow. He became quite persistent and actually annoying. Hence the nickname P.I.T.A. He sent me text after text professing his undying love for me, telling me I was the perfect woman and the only one for him. His texts would start out with, "How is my future wife today?" Very persistent, but I wasn't interested in Darren like he was in me. I would see him out dancing after that and we even danced together a few times (sure, now he wanted to dance with me.) He was a very good dancer but I just had to decline his offers for another date. Good Lord. Imagine what would have happened on the second date after being crowned Miss America on the very first one. That was a very scary thought indeed. With that, Darren was history and I treated him as kindly as I could.

There was another man I met online who I thought had potential but ended up being a disappointment. I chose kindness over letting him know the real reason why I didn't want to see him again. His name was Greg and, like Darren, he was a very nice looking man. We emailed online for a few weeks and finally decided to meet one weekend when we were emailing each other because neither of us had plans, and I had no good excuses to not accept. It was about 8 p.m. on a Saturday night and he told me to pick where we would meet and he would agree. It didn't have to be fancy. Whatever I wanted. Well, what I wanted at that time of night was a soft serve vanilla ice cream cone. I told him to meet me at McDonald's in the town we both lived in.

"McDonald's?!" he asked. "Can't you think of somewhere else besides McDonald's? Maybe we can go somewhere to get a drink?"

No. McDonald's. That's where I wanted to go. Very casual, very public and good soft serve vanilla ice cream. So that is where the two of us ended up on that Saturday night. When Greg arrived in the parking lot, I was interested. He looked just like his photo, which was a good thing. We went inside, got our ice cream (a vanilla cone for me and a chocolate fudge sundae for him), then found a booth. He was surprised I had really ordered the ice cream cone and was eating it in front of him. It seemed that Greg thought it was a bit erotic for a first date, with all that tongue and mouth action going on across the table from him. I truly hadn't thought of it that way but I laughed when he shared that tidbit. Little did I know that there would be some tongue and mouth action between us soon that would make quite a difference in how this story ended. We survived the ice cream cone experience and enjoyed an hour of talking and joking with each other. He seemed like a nice guy and I was really hoping he planned for us to have another date in the near future.

Greg amused me as we walked back out to the parking lot when we had to cross over the drive through lane to get to our cars. The paint for the cross walk was very dim and he promised he would inform management that it needed to be painted brighter so that I would be certain to not get hit by a car when I came back to McDonald's to get my next ice cream cone fix. In fact, he said he was not above coming back that very night and painting it himself just to be certain I was safe. I thought of Greg every time I walked over that crosswalk for years after that. But, forgive me, I should continue telling the story of our first date and why we never had ice cream at McDonald's together again.

Greg called me later that next week and invited me to go to the movies with him on Friday night. We planned to meet at the theatre since we were both coming shortly after work. I was excited for the date and was looking forward to seeing him again. The parking lot was already quite full with all the Friday night dates and family outings. I parked my car and walked quickly over to the theatre to wait for him to arrive as it was starting to rain. It was just a few moments later that he walked up, gave me a hug and bought the tickets for our movie. Since Greg bought the tickets, I offered to buy refreshments. We both got a soft drink and off we went to the theatre to enjoy a movie.

The movie was a good one (although I can't remember now which one it was) and Greg was a true gentleman. After the coming attractions played and our movie began, Greg reached over and took my hand in his. He rubbed my fingers with his, caressed my hand and I enjoyed the attention. This was turning out to be a very nice date, and who knew what would happen, right? Right.

So let's fast forward through the movie, the hand holding, the gentle butterflies in my stomach, the credits rolling and the theatre lights coming on. While very pleasant, nothing worth writing home about in that part, but wait until we got out to the parking lot. That is, unfortunately, where the real action happened and where this story ends.

Greg walked me out to the parking lot and it was still raining. We realized that I had parked at the opposite side of the parking lot than he did, so he would have to run quite a distance in the rain. "Why don't you give me a ride to my car?" he asked with a big smile. Sure, why wouldn't I? We had just shared a wonderful evening together and I was not in a hurry to end it so fast.

Once inside my car and after wiping off our wet faces, we drove over to the far side of the parking lot and, luckily, there was a space available right next to his car. I put my car in park and we sat there in silence for a moment listening to the radio and the rain on the windshield. Somehow I knew what was going to happen next. And I was partly right.

Greg turned to me and I turned towards him. The streetlight was shining softly in through the windshield and the rain was still coming down. 'He's going to kiss me!' I thought. 'Oh, be still, my heart.' I was certain there would be sparks and that this would be the beginning of a wonderful and passionate relationship! Greg leaned in towards me, I leaned in to meet him halfway across the console, and our lips met. This is where the fairy tale ends.

You will have to play along with me now to get the full understanding of this kiss and then it won't even be close to what the real kiss was like. I was expecting a soft, romantic and possibly slightly heated kiss. That's not what I got. My lips were touching Greg's in what I expected would be an almost open mouthed kiss, and his mouth – well, I'm still not sure what he was doing. But if you do this for me now, perhaps you will understand. Pucker your lips and open your mouth just a tiny bit, enough to be able to breathe in through your lips. Almost like you want to whistle a tune. No, really. Come on, pucker up and open your mouth. No one is looking. Now stick the tip of your tongue – just the tip of your tongue – out that little opening so it is flush with your lips, and close your lips down on to your tongue very slightly. Don't let your tongue come out of your mouth any further than the edge of your lips and don't move your lips. Move your tongue very rapidly back and forth and up and down between your teeth while making sure that your lips are tightly wrapped around that vibrating tongue. Stay puckered up, though, and every once in a while you should stop, pause and let that tongue lie there like a fat, wet slug. There you have it. That was the very best kiss that Greg could muster. Okay, you can stop now. People might stare, after all.

I was in shock! 'He must be kidding me,' I thought. 'No one kisses this badly.' I pulled my head away from Greg just far enough to be able to look through one squinting eye into his to see if perhaps he was just messing with me. No, his eyes were closed, his lips were terminally puckered and his tongue was still doing some rapid movement too hard to describe between those lips. I moved in closer again to see if I took control of this kiss, perhaps he would stop this madness? I attempted to engage my lips and tongue skills used to eat ice cream to get him to follow suit and change course. No, he was on a mission, although I'm not sure what he was trying to achieve. 'Should I bite his lips or tongue?' I wondered. Would that make him start kissing me like I craved to be kissed? I was starting to get impatient here and the windows were fogging up.

Greg was still pushing his puckered lips and fat slug of a tongue against my lips and teeth; I was starting to feel nauseous. What if I gagged or threw up on him? How could I ever explain that? I pulled back far enough to make our lips lose contact altogether. Big mistake, because then I could actually see that slug of a tongue doing its little jerky dance between his puckered lips. It took him a second to realize he was kissing air and I was no longer joining in on the moment. Awkward. He opened his eyes and sat back.

"Thank you for a very nice evening, Greg," I said while moving back over to my side of the car.

"What? So soon?" he said.

I nodded shyly and said, "Yes, I need to go."

He thanked me as well and promised to call me again soon to see if I was available to do something else together. You can guess whether that happened or not. How can you date someone who doesn't know how to kiss? My girlfriend told me I should have taught him. Oh, that would have been a nice icebreaker. Greg, you kiss like you have a dying slug in your mouth. Can I teach you how to properly kiss a lady so that we can continue to date? No.

Unfortunately, I had to call it quits with Greg right there and then. He did call and I made excuses. He texted and I was not available. He wanted to have ice cream, go dancing or go to another movie. He would surely want to kiss me again, wouldn't he? All I could think of was the fat wiggling slug between his unmoving puckered lips. I couldn't do it. So, I could have told him that his kissing made me sick, but come on. He was in his mid-40s. Do you think he wasn't aware of how he kissed? Why should I have been the one to bring it up to him? I was sure he either knew it or didn't care. I was not taking that challenge on. We are who we are, and it was up to me to decide if I wanted to move on kindly or hurt his feelings. I chose to be kind. Some things are just better left unsaid.

The final guy I met whose time with me ended in kindness was actually done as his decision, but still with great kindness. He set the standard for how I would personally treat others who I realized weren't the right person for me at that time of my life. Dean was another of my online encounters in the first few years, and we spent a lot of time writing back and forth before meeting each other. He was a little older than me, which didn't bother me in the least. We met at a little taco place (there is a resounding theme of a particular cuisine throughout my stories, right?) and we hit it off right away. Dean was very kind, handsome and witty. I really enjoyed being with him. He had been sober for over 20 years at that time and invited me to attend Alcoholics Anonymous meetings with him. I decided to join him as my previous marriage was to someone addicted to alcohol, and the marriage ended when I gave him the choice of getting help or leaving. He left. This opportunity to attend AA meetings was therapeutic in helping to explain why this addiction was so difficult for many and how giving an ultimatum never works out for the best. There is no winner in an ultimatum, which spending time with Dean helped me understand. I enjoyed the time we shared; however, he was battling some serious demons besides trying to live sober every single day. My life was neat and organized and very sane. Dean's, on the other hand, was not. After we dated for a few months, Dean did something that I believe he did with true affection for me. He told me he couldn't see me anymore because of things he was working through. He said I was a wonderful person and that there was certainly someone out there who I deserved to be with. Although I was hurt initially, it was the best thing in the long run. I knew in my heart that we were too different and what we were sharing was, at best, temporary. Eventually the pain healed, and Dean and I remain friends to this day. He treated me with kindness every single day and let me go on my way with gentleness and affection.

I share this because it's a lesson to take to heart. We often meet people who are in our lives for a moment or for a temporary timeframe. How we let them go is a conscious decision; treating others with respect and kindness when they have treated you in that same manner should be mandatory. As a final note on this subject, I made it a point to reply at least once to every single email that I received from potential suitors and interested Frogs. If I wasn't equally interested in them, I simply thanked them for their email and told them that I didn't believe we would be a suitable match and wished them well. Most Frogs thanked me for answering as they claimed most women just simply ignored the first email. It doesn't cost anything to have compassion and to be kind. When looking for my Prince Charming through these dating years, I met many Frogs who are still friends today. That wouldn't be true if I hadn't been kind in the end with an open heart. I knew how I felt when I was let go with kindness. I wanted others to be treated the same by me. Please choose to be kind. You will always get what you give. 🐸

WHEN LEAST EXPECTED, PRINCE CHARMING MAY JUST APPEAR

I had been participating as an active member on several dating websites off and on for almost nine years. Some experiences in kissing Frogs were pleasant and enjoyable, as you've read in these stories. Other experiences were disappointing, unsavory and hurtful. What happened after a time period of disappointments was that I would make the conscious decision to simply cancel my online memberships, remove my active dating profile from all singles websites and take a much needed dating break, so to speak. That's exactly the point I found myself at once again when my Prince Charming made his entrance. I certainly didn't know he was going to do so. In fact, I was wondering now if he even existed. It was at this point in time I was so disgusted with the Frogs I was kissing, I simply wanted to meet those I had been communicating with and then cancel my account. I was ruling each of them out and then I would be done. It was time to climb out of the dating pond and accept the fact that I was destined to be alone. This happened at least once a year. I would participate online for about nine or 10 months, meet the guys I was interested in, have no luck, and get disgusted and cancel my account. Then after a few months, I'd get bored and start over again. Year after year, after year.

A few months before meeting my Prince Charming, I had a conversation with a dear friend and co-worker on the half day of work before Thanksgiving break began. We were standing in the hallway outside the ladies' restroom getting ready to leave for the holiday and she asked me if I had any big plans. When I told her no, that I would likely take my son, niece and nephew out to breakfast and then spend the day going to the movies with another girlfriend, she asked me, "You aren't dating anyone special?"

I smiled sadly and said, "No, I'm not. But he is out there somewhere. And whatever he is doing this holiday, whoever he is spending it with – he has absolutely no idea how different his life will be after we meet. He will wonder how he ever lived without me." Although I was disenchanted with online dating, somewhere deep in my heart I believed there must surely be someone special still out there waiting for me.

A few months went by, the holidays came and went and, unbeknownst to me, my Prince Charming made his entrance into my life. The first email I received from him was very brief and vague. It simply said, "You have a beautiful smile." Oh, how clever was he? One little sentence of effort to capture my attention? I looked with only mild interest at this man's profile photos (two were posted and looked interesting enough) and read his profile, which was short and to the point, but not very telling. I wondered what his profile name of "Unglaubich" meant. So I Googled the word and discovered it meant "unbelievable" in German. 'Hmmm, okay then – that's clever,' I thought. I wrote back to Mr. Unbelievable with a short message of my own: "Your smile isn't too bad, either. Unbelievable, in fact." Several days went by without another email and I moved along. It was time to weed out the losers and get off that dating site. I was ready for a much-needed break and was ready to crawl out of the pond.

In the meantime, however, I was corresponding with another man who had captured my interest. Attractive, funny and in my sights as possibly date worthy. He wanted to meet me very soon, he said. However, I had plans that coming weekend. My girlfriend was having her birthday party, which of course meant a pre-birthday celebration with the girls on Friday night dancing, followed by another birthday gathering on Saturday with lots of friends. There would be no time for dates that weekend.

Mid-week I received another email from Mr. Unbelievable. He wanted to get together for lunch if I had the time that week. 'What the heck,' I thought. 'Let's get it over with so I can mark him off the list and move on with canceling my account.' I held absolutely no hopes that he would be any different from anyone else I had met. We made plans for a lunch date on Friday but I knew there was a great possibility that it wouldn't turn out well. There were too many Frogs in my recent past who had turned out to be simply un-kissable.

But then I got an email from the other guy I mentioned above. This other Frog held my interest both in written communication and in the few phone conversations we'd had. I hadn't talked with Mr. Unbelievable yet, so I felt more connected to this particular Frog. And he wanted to meet me for lunch on Friday, the same day I had agreed to have lunch with Mr. Unbelievable. What's a girl to do? Well, the only thing possible. I cancelled the Friday lunch date with my future Prince Charming and agreed to go to lunch with another Frog. Yes, Mr. Unbelievable was disappointed when I told him through email that something had come up and I would have to reschedule. I certainly didn't tell him that it was his competition! Through email we agreed to meet for lunch on Tuesday of the following week and I gave him my phone number. He said he would call me over the weekend and we could make our plans to get together. I still was not very interested in Mr. Unbelievable; I was much more interested in my lunch date on Friday with someone who I thought I might truly like. Remember, once again, I found myself at the point where all I wanted to do was mark these Frogs off my list and settle into my singleness. I was completely fed up with kissing Frogs.

Our Friday lunch date came and I was a little nervous as I walked into the restaurant where I was meeting Mr. Not My Prince Charming. His name was Chuck and I recognized him sitting in the booth of the New York style deli immediately. He got up from the table and kissed my cheek. He was sweet, nice looking with curly black hair, and very tall. 'So far so good,' I thought. Until he started talking, that is. The problem with Chuck was that he simply couldn't say one sentence without using extremely profane language. He never uttered one foul word during our phone conversations; however, during this lunch date he was absolutely disgusting and obnoxious. He said the A word, the B word, the C word (yes), the D word – there is no E word that I'm aware of – and even the F word! He combined the G word with the D word and even jumped the alphabet to the S words. This went completely against my grain because although I may say a cuss word here or there, I surely wasn't going to do it in a crowded restaurant like Chuck was doing!

"I'm going to wash your mouth out with soap, mister," I said to Chuck. This didn't get my point across, no ma'am. I thought it was a pretty good clue that he was offending me. Evidently this Frog didn't have that much sense about him. Instead, he continued spouting off the profanities of the alphabet throughout our lunch. I was embarrassed, to say the very least, as patrons at the other tables could hear the conversation. "Chuck, really. Do you kiss your mother with that mouth?" I asked. Again, no clue. Unfortunately, it didn't faze him and I was never so happy for a lunch hour to end. As we stood in front of our cars, he asked if I wanted to see him again. There was no reason to mince words. "Not really, Chuck. I'm offended by your language. I simply don't use profanity like you do and obviously it's something you are comfortable with."

Chuck seemed surprised and replied, "Why didn't you tell me, Rose?" Sigh.

As I left that lunch date shared with Potty Mouth Chuck that Friday afternoon and drove back to work, I was looking forward to writing this one off. Additionally, I was hoping to get through the last planned date with Mr. Unbelievable so that I could put an end to this nonsense. I truly needed a break from kissing Frogs. It was clearly time to remove myself from online dating and focus on more positive distractions. Like waxing my car or repainting my walls. I could think of so many things more exciting to do than continuing with internet dating. I even had visions of spending the remaining days of my life living with another single girlfriend and becoming old maids together. It had gotten that desperately sad.

That evening as I was getting ready to go out with my girlfriends for the pre-birthday celebration, my phone rang. I was in the middle of fixing my hair and had to stop to answer the phone. "Is this Rose?" the caller asked in a voice heavy with accent.

"It is indeed," I replied.

My mystery caller that evening was none other than Mr. Unbelievable. He was phoning to confirm our date on Tuesday and express his disappointment that we weren't able to meet earlier that day. Of course, he thought I had cancelled due to a meeting at work and not because I was having lunch with Mister Potty Mouth. I felt a little guilty about that, but I wasn't quite sure I wanted to expend more effort to meet one more Frog out in the dating pond. Even if he was Mr. Unbelievable with an interesting accent. 'Perhaps I should just cancel now and call it quits,' I thought. But those weren't the words that came out of my mouth.

Instead, I heard myself saying, "If you aren't busy on Sunday, we could meet up for an hour or so in the afternoon. If we can still stand the sight of each other after that meeting, we can go ahead and have our lunch date on Tuesday. Agreed?"

He agreed, I told him where to meet me Sunday, and as he began talking a little more, I cut him off. A little rudely, I might add. "Hey, I would really like to talk some more, but I need to get ready to go out with the girls. I'm already running late. Can we talk on Sunday?"

And that was the first phone conversation with Mr.

Unbelievable. Short, sweet and to the point. Sunday brought a whole new conversation, which was much, much longer in length.

I could share the happenings of the night out on Friday with the girls or the fun birthday party for my girlfriend on Saturday. But that isn't the real story here. It began on Sunday afternoon a little before 3 p.m. when I pulled into the parking lot of a popular – yes, Mexican – restaurant where I asked Mr. Unbelievable to meet me. For this simple meeting, I was dressed casually and comfortably with no fuss. When I say casual, I mean really casual. I wore black sweat pants, a T-shirt with a jacket over it, tennis shoes and my hair was pulled up. I did have my makeup on and some jewelry, but I was by no means interested in impressing anyone. I just needed to check him off the list, disqualify him like all the others and get my profile deleted on the dating websites. So there I was, meeting him at another of my favorite restaurants. At least I should enjoy it, right?

However, as I pulled in to the restaurant parking lot, I saw that the cars of two of my girlfriends were in the parking lot. None other than the birthday girl and one of our friends. They clearly didn't get enough partying for the birthday girl during the two previous nights out and were meeting up for a margarita on Sunday afternoon. There was no way in hell I was meeting a blind date in an establishment that some of my girlfriends were having drinks in. That would be even worse than just having a blind date. I simply had to find somewhere else for us to meet, and quick!

Looking across the street, I saw a chicken place called Wings 'N' More. Frantically I dialed Mr. Unbelievable on my phone and asked him if we could change the place we were meeting. I told him where to meet me and he explained that he had driven to the Mexican restaurant location in the center of town by accident and was running late. He would be there in about 10 minutes. I took that opportunity to drive across the street and park in the Wings 'N' More parking lot, where I watched and waited for my Sunday date to arrive. My expectations were not very high. I simply wanted to mark him off the list and move on.

I saw Mr. Unbelievable drive into the parking lot in his truck. As I climbed out of my car, I waited for this man – the man I intended to be my final online date for quite some time to come – to park. As he walked towards me, I felt butterflies start in my stomach. This here was an attractive man! "Rose, I presume?" he asked as he extended his hand.

"Robert, I presume?" I playfully returned as I reached out and shook the hand of Mr. Unbelievable.

Now I can't recall every subject we talked about or all that we shared that afternoon. I know that we both first drank a beer and then we switched to iced tea. We didn't order food, although he offered and we each got up from the table one time to use the restroom. We sat in the bar area and it was easy and comfortable. He asked me questions, I shared stories. I asked him questions and he shared stories. He was from Switzerland (hence the accent) and I shared that I was from Montana. Neither one of us looked at our watches or our cell phones; but I promise we sat on those wooden benches long enough for my butt to get sore. Finally, I looked at my watch and was very surprised to see that three and a half hours had passed by like a flash, and I had enjoyed every moment of it!

After paying the check, Robert walked me out to the parking lot and as we stood at the back of my car, he asked, "Well, should we continue with our lunch date on Tuesday? Do you think we can stand the sight of each other?"

I smiled, he smiled back and I said, "Yes, let's have lunch on Tuesday." He hugged me goodbye and our first encounter ended on a very positive note.

As Robert left the parking lot, I texted the birthday girl to see if they were still having margaritas across the street. She replied yes, so I drove back to the Mexican restaurant to join the girls. They knew I had a blind date that day and as I sat down and ordered a margarita, they asked me how it went. My poor girlfriends had heard every story written in this book and then some; therefore, they expected to hear another horror story. I smiled and said, "It went really well. I like him." And I smiled again as I waited for my margarita.

Tuesday came and it was time for our first real date, the replacement lunch date for the cancelled Friday date. We met at a barbeque place near my work and we arrived in the parking lot at the same time. We were both dressed in work clothes rather than our casual clothes from Sunday, and I believe Robert was pleasantly surprised at the difference in my appearance. Instead of sweats, a T-shirt and tennis shoes, I was in a dress with high heels. Robert was a little more nervous during that date than he had been on Sunday and I found it endearing. Neither one of us ate very much at lunch at all. The hour passed all too quickly and soon it was time to go back to work. He then asked me if I had plans for Friday night. I shared that I certainly did not and was very happy that we would be having another date in just a few short days.

We started a routine that evening of talking on the phone every night at bedtime. Robert would call me from his house south of town, which was 35 miles from where I lived north of town. We would talk for about an hour and during these conversations, we really got to know each other. Our communication was easy and he made me laugh. That is never a bad thing! Neither one of us ever wanted to hang up the phone after only an hour but since it was a school night, we would always make sure to do so even though we hated saying goodnight.

Our Friday night date finally came. Robert planned to pick me up at my office, as it was the mid-way point between both of our houses; although neither of us had been to the other's home yet. When five o'clock came, I rushed down the hallway to freshen up my makeup. I was waiting for the phone call to let me know that he was right around the corner so that I could walk outside to meet him. Butterflies and excitement! Who was this girl who felt this way after wanting so badly to be done with internet dating? Where had this guy come from? Robert called to say he was pulling in to my office complex. I rushed out of our five story building on that Friday night ready to start our date. As I walked into the parking lot, there he stood, smiling – leaning against his shiny silver Mercedes (not his truck this time), with feet crossed at the ankles, holding a single, long stemmed red rose. Wasn't I happy that he was sweet enough to bring one single rose and not the whole flipping bouquet?! How very romantic this man was!

As we got settled in his car, I was holding the rose in my hand while feeling nervous and giddy. "I want to play a song for you," Robert said. We were just pulling out of the building complex when he pushed play on the CD system. The music started, I heard the first notes and said, "I know this song!" and then the words echoed throughout the car. I was silent the entire time the song played. Frank and Nancy Sinatra sang a duet with the first words bringing warmth to my face and a smile in my heart:

"I know I stand in line until you think you have the time

To spend an evening with me

And if we go someplace to dance, I know that there's a chance

You won't be leaving with me

And afterwards we drop into a quiet little place and have a drink or two

And then I go and spoil it all by saying something stupid like 'I love you.'"

Imagine my thoughts at that very moment! What an impression to make on my heart. Our date was perfect. Dinner at a wonderful restaurant out by the lake followed by drinks at a little Mexican (of course) restaurant back near the office where my car was parked. Neither of us wanted the night to end – but it did. This night was followed by many more dates – lunch once a week, spending nights on the weekends together and long phone conversations each evening as we lied in our own beds before going to sleep. We just clicked. While our personalities were not similar at all, our core values, life goals and experiences were very similar. We brought out the best in each other.

Robert didn't have to ask me to marry him. We just knew that it would be the proper course for our lives to take and we moved in that direction naturally. We met on February 28 and we were married on June 26 – less than four months from our first date at Wings 'N' More. I knew after two weeks that this was my Prince Charming and we would make a life together. It hit me when I was working out at the gym listening to my iPod and the song "At Last" by Etta James played in my ears. I knew then that he was the one as I sat there on the weight machine with tears in my eyes listening to these words:

"At last my love has come along

My lonely days are over and

Life is like a song, oh yeah

At last the skies above are blue

My heart was wrapped up in clover

The night I looked at you."

Robert will claim that he knew I was the one on that first Tuesday at lunch – our first real date together. As they say – when it's right, it's right. You just know. I had waited nine years to find my Prince Charming and it was very close to not ever happening. Imagine if I'd given up just one week earlier. Robert was only active on the online dating website for less than two weeks when he met me. We were very close to not meeting each other at all; never mind that I was simply just trying to get him marked off of the Loser list so I could delete my dating profile and stop with the nonsense of kissing Frogs.

I would like to make it clear that those close to me

thought I had lost my ever-loving mind when I let them know Robert and I had decided to get married after only a few months of knowing each other. I had been single for nine years with no serious relationships. They simply weren't ready for this idea and thought we were rushing things. My friend who worked in Human Resources even asked if there was any way I could get Robert's social security number so that we could run a background check on him. She wanted to make certain that he wasn't just looking for someone to make his life easier. "After all," she stated, "you have a military retirement with full benefits, a great job, decent 401k balance and a nice house." Perhaps he was trying to make his life easier by marrying me? I countered by listing all of the great things Robert brought to the relationship. He was a great package as well! We were very well balanced and a background check wasn't necessary. Likewise, when Robert shared with his golfing buddies that he had met the woman he planned to marry, they tried to talk him out of it and strongly encouraged him to stay single and not ruin a good thing. We both listened to our hearts with the voice of reality interjecting when necessary, and have never regretted that decision for one moment.

Without the possibility afforded by online dating, Robert and I would never have met. He lived south of town, I lived north. Robert golfed, I bowled. I went out dancing with my girlfriends, he didn't go out except to the golf course in his neighborhood. Our lives would be very different today if it had not been for his email complimenting my smile and my willingness to kiss just one more Frog. Think of that, just one more Frog. We are blessed in this life to share our days, nights and years together. We both know our chance at meeting was purely fate and we take every day as a blessed gift. We were closer to never meeting than we both actually realized. Considering kissing just one more Frog presented the opportunity that eventually became Us.

Is our life perfect together? As perfect as any relationship beginning mid-life can be, yes. We both brought our own drama in pieces of luggage when we met; however, they were small enough pieces to fit in the compartment above our heads and below the seat in front of us. Nothing needed to be checked through the gate agent. No relationship is without its periods of growth, compromise and learning how to bring out the best in each other. With that comes the desire to bring out the best in ourselves and be the best partner we can be to each other. That being said, we have incorporated some very important things in our routine that have made our lives more blessed as each year passes.

We have lunch together every Wednesday at a quaint Italian restaurant, we enjoy date night every single Friday (either as a couple or inviting other couples to join in), and we go to a movie and brunch almost every Sunday morning. We don't call each other by our first names (unless we are not happy with the other person at that moment, which never lasts very long). He calls me Sweetheart and Honey Bunny. I call him Love and Mr. Gloor (mainly for our dog as he didn't want to be called Daddy). We get up every weekday morning at 4:45 a.m., we make the bed together, work out together for an hour and then text each other when we get to work without fail. He calls me when he gets off work and I call him when I get close to home. I still bowl and Robert still golfs. We have yet to take up the other person's sport … maybe when we retire. Robert brings me fresh flowers every week and sometimes I have multiple bouquets in bloom in the house at one time. We hold hands often and always when walking in public. We spoil each other. The only holiday we have never celebrated is Valentine's Day. We choose to celebrate our love and relationship the other 364 days of the year. Every day is a blessing, every month brings something new to celebrate and every year behind us is full of smiles, laughter, warmth and happiness. We focus on the positives. We cherish our life together and are thankful we took the chance on internet dating. We bring out the best in each other and forgive the other person for the rest. Our only regret is that we didn't meet thirty years earlier. But I don't believe we would appreciate where we are together today if we hadn't lived those hard years of our lives apart.

Yes, I've kissed a lot of Frogs in my life – most of them during the nine years I spent as an active member on dating websites. As I've shared in this book, some of those Frogs were very memorable for good reasons, while others simply can't be forgotten (even if I try, and now even if you try as well). I'm thankful I took the chance to explore dating websites although I truly held no hopes of finding my Prince Charming or ever marrying again. Life truly is full of such possibilities. There are many Frogs in the pond and, yes, unfortunately there are Toads in there as well. If you or someone you know are still holding out hope in finding the love of your life, or are hoping to meet Prince Charming, take my experiences shared within these pages to heart and learn what you can from them. Give internet dating a chance for the first time or perhaps the tenth. I encourage you to get back out in the pond and keep searching for your Princess or Prince Charming. I truly believe that special person is out there waiting just for you. They are on the next lily pad, around that corner, waiting for you to arrive. Beyond that, I leave you with only two words of advice.

Pucker up.